The Music In My Rearview Mirror

Shelia Shipley Biddy

ISBN-10: 1500978280
ISBN-13: 978-1500978280

DEDICATION

This book is dedicated to all who hold a dream in their heart and dare to believe it can come true.

CONTENTS

ACKNOWLEDGMENTS

How do I begin to thank so many people who have raised, encouraged, impacted, and believed in me, even when I doubted myself? If I leave anyone out in this story it is only due to the time and space it would take to include so many wonderful people that have graced my life in so many incredible ways.

First, I have to thank God for always being there for me. In the darkest hours before the dawn when there seemed to be no hope, to intensive care rooms and life-saving doctors sent as angels to save my life, I pray my life has been a blessing to Him. I ask forgiveness for the bad thoughts and bad language I have been known to express, and I hope those words never caused anyone to doubt my faith.

To Pauline and Sam, my mother and grandmother, I thank you for being strong Kentucky women whose examples of hard work and strong faith molded me into the independent woman I am.

To Bennie, who loved me first and gave me my only son, Michael, you made me a stronger person because you believed in me long before I believed in myself,

To Michael, who often challenged a mother's love, and who gave me my only grandson, Kyle. I *do* love you and I am proud of the man you have grown up to be.

To my grandson, Kyle, you are the love of my life. I am so proud of you and only wish I could see you more often.

To John Dorris, who gave me my first job in the music business and taught me a lot about life outside my Kentucky home. I admire your faith and treasure your lifetime of friendship.

To Paul Lovelace who taught me that it is ok to make decisions I am happy with. I don't have to please everyone else. You gave me the best advice I ever got about those crossroads, and I wore out that paperback copy of *The World's Greatest Salesman.* Like you, I have given it away many times throughout my career

To Fred Foster, for your incredible wisdom—and for the phone call to a doctor more than thirty-five years ago. You saved my life and taught me the *magic* of the music.

To Joe Galante, for teaching me about the *business* of music. You taught me to love the music first and to build a plan of action that ended with a successful result. You also taught me to be tough. I will always be most grateful to you for allowing me to "do radio promotion" and for teaching me that the marketing of an artist first starts with radio.

To Jimmy Bowen, for being the most colorful character I ever met in this business. You threw me into the water and told me to swim, and swim I did. You scared others, protected me, made me a vice president, and changed the course of history—for me and so many others, especially women. You taught me, "to take care of the music and the music will always take care of you."

To Bruce Hinton and Tony Brown, who supported and believed in me, and allowed me the autonomy to make decisions that changed the lives of countless employees and artists. We had the best of times and the greatest of memories.

To all the country radio programmers who took my calls, replied to an email, and played my music, thank you.

To Tatum Hauck Allsep, we go back to the days of MCA when you were still in college, and now your vision and tenacity has launched Music Health Alliance. I am so proud to be part of this inspiring new company. You have already helped so many creative people with health care issues. I am proud to join *your* team.

To Lisa Wysocky: how can I thank you for providing your expertise to edit this book and guide me in filling in the holes of my life story? I will be forever grateful to you for your wisdom and guidance.

To Ken's birth children (Crystal, Daniel, Dena, and Amanda) who accepted me as their "Nashville Momma" and have loved and embraced me with open arms. How can I ever begin to tell you how much your love means to me?

Most of all, I have to thank Ken Biddy. Some say I am easy to love, while others say if they didn't know me, they might be afraid of me. I have heard that more than once. Part of that is because I present an exterior that doesn't let many people in. I am hard on the outside and soft on the inside, and a contradiction of emotions rolled up in a hard-working woman. In some ways I am trusting. In other ways, I don't trust at all. As the old country adage says, "A child twice burned is afraid of fire."

Scott Borchetta is currently CEO of Big Machine Label Group (home to superstar Taylor Swift) but once worked for me at MCA. Several years ago, he told a promoter who asked about me that "You either have to work for Shelia or be part of her family if you are ever to know what she is really like." He nailed that right on the head. I am an extremely private person (most of the time). Ken tugged on that soft spot inside of me the very first time we met. He is tough as nails and often quick to judge. Even after he swore never to marry again, he saw something he trusted in me and for that I am eternally grateful. He is my strength and defender, my friend and my ally in life's storms. While we don't agree on everything, we do agree that we are better together than apart.

We have now walked side by side for twenty-one years and I pray we have another twenty-one years to discover all the things we have not yet figured out. If we don't figure it out here, then maybe we can get some answers when we get to Heaven. Thank you, Ken, for choosing to love me and for being tolerant of all my short-comings. I love you from the bottom of my country heart and soul.

FOREWORD

Shelia Shipley Biddy and I have a lot in common. We are both women, we are both in a business dominantly ruled by men. We both love music, and we both have been successful in a career we love. This all makes us very blessed and fortunate women.

Being a woman, it takes a lot of hard work and long hours to get ahead and maintain the level of success we desire. But man, it's worth it! I am so glad that challenge didn't slow Shelia down one bit.

Shelia worked twenty-one #1 singles for me. As I've always said, it takes a team, not just one person to make those #1's happen. I'm so glad I was on that team with Shelia. She worked hard and went to bat to make sure those songs were hits! I sure do appreciate all her hard work.

When you read this book, you'll learn about all her hard work, and all the amazing folks she got to work with. I know she has some great stories for you! Plus, because of Shelia, huge doors have opened for other women to take on the music business.

Thanks, Shelia. We need more like you, but I think God broke the mold when He made you!

Love,

Reba McEntire

INTRODUCTION

It was during a Country Radio Seminar in the mid-1990s that I first came into contact with Shelia Shipley Biddy, and I remember the moment as if it was yesterday. I had been working at WDKN in Dickson, Tennessee—a truly "small market" radio station, but one I took a great deal of pride in being involved with. At that point in my career, I desperately wanted to be taken seriously by people who were involved in the inner workings of the music business.

At one point during the conference, several people stepped into an elevator in Nashville's Renaissance Hotel. Two of the people were Shelia Shipley Biddy and me. A conversation began concerning Lee Ann Womack, who was one of Shelia's marquee acts on Decca Records. Though I was not affiliated with a reporting station, Shelia was very gracious and kind to someone she didn't have to be that way to.

Over the years I have had the pleasure of working with Shelia on various projects, and her kindness is always there. Shelia grew up under a great deal of hardship in rural Kentucky and early on, many in the music industry treated her as if she had reached her glass ceiling in low-level secretarial and receptionist jobs. Shelia persevered, however, and made history as senior vice president of the promotion department of MCA Records in Nashville. Under her leadership MCA became the "it" label in Music City. In just a few short years, an amazing 139 number one singles were promoted to the top by Shelia and her staff.

In 1993, when Decca Records was resurrected, Shelia became the first female head of a major record label in Nashville. Her appointment to Decca was history making, for sure. But she dug in deep, led by example, and always took time to say a kind word, or give encouragement to those following in her giant footsteps. That meant a lot to someone like me. It still does.

The career accomplishments that Shelia has enjoyed stand with those from such iconic figures in Nashville as Mae Axton, Jo Walker Meador, Connie Bradley, and Donna Hilley. And, just as she is an influence to women in the business, any of us can learn from her amazing story of determination and hard work. Just ask Royce Risser at Universal or Scott Borchetta at Big Machine, two of the most influential people in the promotion business today. Who first hired them? You guessed it! Shelia Shipley Biddy.

But, there's more to her story than just a legendary career. Shelia Shipley Biddy is a loving wife, mother, daughter, and friend. She has endured poverty, neglect, abuse, a life-threatening illness, and much more. In the pages of this book, you'll cheer, you'll laugh, and you'll even cry at a childhood that was far from the carefree existence that most of us had in small-town America. Hers is a success story, not just about country music, but about life. So get ready to be inspired, no matter what mountain you currently face.

Chuck Dauphin
Billboard Magazine

PREFACE

Whenever I speak on a panel, I am asked when I plan to write my autobiography. After all, my career has spanned almost four decades and I have seen a lot of changes in this business we call music. A lot of people seem to be interested in how I got into the business, and how I reached the pinnacle of success by running Decca Records in the 1990s.

In the process, I had some amazing experiences. I never in a million years thought I would look up from the island in my kitchen where I was preparing dinner to see Jimmy Buffett strolling in. I had been at MCA Records for a few years and was giving a dinner for my promotion staff at my Brentwood home. This was something I often did when they were in town for meetings. Earlier in the day I had been informed that I had been promoted to senior vice president of promotion. MCA chairman Bruce Hinton wanted to announce it to the staff that night at dinner and wanted me to keep it quiet until we all got together. Bruce arrived shortly after the staff, and carried Dom Perignon in hand. A few minutes later, my staff and I were standing around the island in my kitchen fixing drinks when my doorbell rang

Bruce said, “I’ll get it.”

That surprised me. Why would Bruce Hinton want to answer my front door? I found out moments later when he reentered the kitchen with Jimmy Buffett.

“Here’s my first surprise,” said Bruce, referring to Buffett. “The second surprise is that we have just named Shelia the senior vice president of promotion for MCA. Cheers!”

Surrounded by Jimmy Buffett, Bruce Hinton, my husband, Ken Biddy; and nine of my promotion staff, I felt blessed beyond being blessed. I was beaming with pride. And why not? My dreams had all come true. I was at the top of my game and the top of my industry. Little did I know, but that night was only the beginning of the success I was to achieve in the years that followed.

The story of my career, however, cannot be told without starting at the very beginning. If you had known me as a shy, insecure young girl growing up in a small southern Kentucky town, you would not have expected me to become president of a huge Nashville record company. The many challenges I overcame in my early life, however, strengthened me into a person who could handle the challenges of such a leadership position.

We all learn by challenge and opportunity, and the outcome depends on the choices we make in dealing with such adversity. That's the story you will read within these pages. That is my story. I wish I could tell you that I had a plan from the beginning of my life to accomplish lofty dreams and become a leader in the music industry. But such was not the case. Even with written plans, life has a way of changing those strategies. I do know that God opened doors that I could not open myself, and I am forever grateful.

I am living proof that a small town girl can achieve wondrous things through hard work, strong faith, determination, and opportunity. I believe there are crossroads throughout our life where we make decisions that will affect us until we reach the next life-changing moment—that next crossroad of decision. That crossroad can be a job opportunity, health crisis, friend, or mentor whose words of wisdom dramatically impact our direction. For that reason, you will notice a similar thread in all the crossroads I have been through on my journey.

I look back and recall many forks in the road throughout my career and private life. Each decision affected the next leg of my journey. While every decision I made may not have been the right one at the time, it did help me grow into the person I am today. This book is a look in my rear view mirror. It is a reflection of where I have been, the people who have impacted my life, and where I am headed until I reach the next crossroad.

Shelia Shipley Biddy

CHAPTER 1

The King of Country Music

I remember the crunch and smell of sawdust under my feet as I headed toward the arena. It was the first time I had attended the Houston Livestock Show and Rodeo, and my heart raced as I became engulfed in the excitement of the evening. As part of a major record label, I was there to support one of our acts. My job usually involved lots of phone and desk time, so it was always a treat to go out to see an artist perform. But as performances go, this was something else.

The nervousness of the horses rippled through the air like an electric current as cowboys and cowgirls prepared to mount and perform their opening night ride. The backstage area and tunnels that led into the arena were crowded with workers, and with musicians who were preparing to take the stage. Everyone was running on adrenaline as they worked their way to their appointed places. As I stepped through a back doorway and onto the arena floor, I was suddenly surrounded by seventy-one thousand people––all of whom were eagerly waiting for the night to begin. The show was just moments away.

Soon, the lights went down and a lone spotlight riveted upon a young girl in a cowboy hat as she took the stage to sing the "The Star Spangled Banner," and seventy-one thousand people stood to pay tribute to our great country. Tears welled in my eyes, and I was overcome with emotion. As the young girl's voice echoed with her finale, a shout went up from the crowd. Horses and riders began to file into the arena, kicking up sawdust as the multi-colored flags they carried waved in the breeze. And then they were gone.

Next, a pickup truck carrying musicians careened into the arena and toward the stage. The crowd cheered and stomped their feet. The arena slowly grew dark and shouts from the fans grew louder. Suddenly, the spotlight shined to a corner of the arena where a lone rider entered on a magnificent brown stallion. He circled the arena at a gallop, once, then twice, as shouts went up from the crowd. Suddenly, he turned and headed toward the stage where he dismounted and climbed the stairs. As the first notes of the song "Fireman" began to play, George Strait strapped on his guitar and began to sing the words seventy-one thousand people had been waiting for weeks to hear. The King of Country Music was home on the throne at the Houston Livestock Show and Rodeo. The arena's jumbotron reflected George's image bigger than life, and each time he flashed a smile the crowd went into a frenzy.

Ninety minutes of hits later, George bid us all good night, walked down the stairs and mounted his horse. Around the arena once, then twice, then he asked his horse to rear up. Then he took off his Stetson hat and threw it high into the crowd. With that he was gone, and the crowd again went crazy.

Once more, I became overwhelmed with pride as I wiped tears from my eyes. As I headed backstage to find George Strait and his crew, I reminded myself for the thousandth time how blessed I was to work in a business that I loved so much. But for you to know just how blessed, I need to start at the beginning.

CHAPTER 2

The Beginning

I was born October 2, 1952, in Dr. Miller's office over Bentley's Five & Dime Store in Scottsville, Kentucky. As it was just six years after the conclusion of World War II, I entered a world very different to the world I live in today. A few years before I came into this world, wives and mothers had given up their factory jobs for men who had returned home from war. Those men came back to claim their "rightful position" as bread-winners and heads of households. Back then, men took on the roles they believed God and society intended for them. I am sure some women struggled with the loss of their short-term individuality, while others may have relished the idea of having a man to provide for their needs. Those women looked ahead to a future that held the promise of home making, child rearing, and little else.

Such was my mother's dream. Such was mine as a little girl. But as I grew older, my dreams began to change. I wanted what my mother wanted, but I also wanted more. I wanted it all. I wanted to be more than Mrs. Somebody. I wanted to be important to the world—someone who mattered, who had their own name and made a difference, no matter how small. I wanted a career to call my own while also attaining a loving home life. It was a nice dream, but during my formative years it seemed impossible that it would ever become reality.

• • •

I grew up the middle child of Pauline and Robert Davis. When Momma and Daddy married, he was twenty-four and she was fourteen. That was the way it was done in Southern small town USA then. Daddy returned from World War II in January of 1946. He had been part of the 11th Airborne Division, and fought in New

Guinea and the Philippine Islands. Not yet eighteen years old, my dad had left the Kentucky farm where he was raised to join the army. There, he was trained as a glider pilot and paratrooper who jumped behind and into Japanese encampments entrenched in the Pacific.

As a child, I loved to hear the stories of fighting in those tropical islands, of the intense heat, and mosquitos that were large enough to carry lanterns during pitch black nights walking guard duty. Daddy's stories fascinated my older brother, Shelby, and me. He painted pictures of faraway places filled with mystery and intrigue. We often begged him to tell us stories and had no idea how hard it was for him to talk about the war and the atrocities he had witnessed. When I grew older, I discovered that he was haunted by the faces of the dead men he had seen.

Sometimes, late at night, Daddy told us about the terrible things he witnessed. Once, his platoon scouted out a Japanese prison camp on the island. His unit was assigned to rescue prisoners who had been held captive there since the war began. While the ground forces quietly approached from the outside, paratroopers silently jumped inside this Japanese prison camp. The paratroopers' goal was to secure the gate and open it for the ground troops.

Daddy described the prisoners he found: skinny, old men with long white beards and tattered clothing. When the troops arrived, the prisoners leapt to their feet with cheers and tears, because they realized they would soon be free again. They kissed the soldier's feet and hands, knowing that years of prayers had finally been answered. The memories of those stories echo through the corridors of my mind to this very day. Daddy was my John Wayne. To me, he was bigger than life.

Daddy was born in Shelbyville, Tennessee, the son of Edward and Tilley Davis. He had five brothers and sisters: Floyd, Hasson, Clarene, Lola, and Lena. Momma said that when they first met, Daddy drove an old green army Jeep, and was so handsome that he took her breath away. Looking at his early photos, I can believe it. I always thought he and Momma looked like movie stars. To me, my dad and mom were the most handsome couple in the world. He loved baseball, drag racing, wrestling, non-filtered camel cigarettes, and country music—especially the two Hanks: Hank

Snow and Hank Williams, Sr. But most of all, Daddy loved me. I was sure of it, even though I can't ever recall hearing him speak the words. He just made me feel loved in a million different ways.

Daddy made his living cutting timber. He was such a good logger that people called him if they had a difficult tree that needed cutting. Folks in our parts say he could put a tree on the ground exactly where he intended it to fall, and could figure the number of board feet in the tree just by looking at it.

My dad always smelled of sawdust and cigarette smoke when he came home at the end of the day. Even as an adult, so many years removed from those dusky evenings when I waited for him to come home from work, the smell of sawdust takes me back to those late evenings waiting for his return. Shelby and I always waited for him under the big walnut tree at the bottom of our hill. We watched for his log truck, and as soon as we saw it turn off Highway 31-E and head for home, we grew excited.

The reason for our excitement was that Daddy often spoiled us by bringing home treats. So every evening we watched for him, never knowing what he might have. Sometimes he brought us orange or banana flavored Popsicles, fried cherry pies, chocolate snowballs, or hostess cupcakes.

Other nights, he slowly got out of the truck and gently picked up a towel that moved in his hands as he opened it for us to see. Inside might be baby squirrels or baby raccoons that had been in trees he had cut. He'd bring them home and Momma cared for them. She had a "doll bottle," to mix up milk in, and she fed the babies with the bottle or eye dropper until they could open their eyes and eat on their own. We had Squeaky the Squirrel, and Jimmy and Timmy were raccoons. Squeaky sometimes climbed up the curtains to hide, or play with us. Jimmy and Timmy were great fun, too. Before our well was dug, Momma and Daddy walked to the spring about a quarter mile from our house to get water. Our raccoons loped right along with us, played in the creek branch, and caught crawfish. I used to think it was funny to watch them wash their fish, even though they had just pulled them out of the water.

My mother was born Pauline Powell and was the daughter of Sallie Anne and Baxter Rutledge Powell. She had one brother, Baxter Powell, Jr. Momma is one of the strongest people I know. Of all the people I have known or worked with, I admire her most of all. She never sat behind a big desk, nor did she hold countless degrees. But, she has a special kind of wisdom and a love deep inside that helped her overcome the odds she faced. No matter what curve ball life threw her, Momma always caught it. She was our oak tree in a life filled with storms.

There are a lot of things in life that I am unsure of, but one thing I know is that Momma loved Daddy with all her heart—maybe too much. When Shelby and I were small, Momma was a home-maker. I remember watching her work all day around the house, mowing the yard, working in the garden, and doing laundry. By late afternoon, I watched her walk a half-mile to the spring and carry buckets of water back to the house so she could take a bath and get ready for Daddy to come home. She put on makeup, fixed her hair, put on a skirt, and tried very hard to make sure he always had whatever he wanted.

I was small, but I remember thinking that Daddy must be pretty special for her to go to all that trouble. I look back now and wonder if she tried too hard. She had many philosophies about life, and one of those was when two people argue, they should always make up before they go to sleep. She said, "If you don't, the problem will only be bigger in the morning." I swore that when I grew up, that too, would be my motto. Little did I know that it takes two people willing to do that, not just one.

Late at night, Momma held me in her arms and sang to me. I remember "Twinkle, Twinkle, Little Star" and "When You Wish Upon a Star," and it was as if an angel was rocking me to sleep. I grew up believing with all my heart that wishes do come true. She sang me all the popular songs of the day, from Jim Reeves to Eddy Arnold to Bing Crosby. Momma had such a beautiful voice, and I always felt safe in her arms and recall the beating of her heart as she rocked me to sleep.

Sometimes, when she wasn't singing, she looked out the window and pointed to the moon and stars, and told me stories about how God put them up there in the sky to give the darkness light. Momma believed in the miracle of prayer and (thankfully) instilled that same belief in me. She believed that God's work is often done somewhere other than the church, and I have found that to be true. She prayed for a lot of people, and when others asked her about her faith, she stopped what she was doing to talk to them about it. Many people never attend church and only know God through the kindness of strangers, or those who work beside them each and every day. But if they met my Momma, they would feel the kindness of God pouring through her. She had an unconditional love for her family that was reflected despite our missteps and bad decisions. Momma has always been there for me.

My momma also had the softest heart of anyone I have ever met. She never turned away a stray cat or dog, goat or bird. She was always there to embrace and save the smallest of creatures, and continues to do so to this very day. Once, our cat came to the house with a huge bullfrog in its mouth. The frog was lifeless, its tummy was split open, and its intestines were showing. Momma, however, felt a heartbeat, so it was time to save the frog. She took a needle and thread, pushed the small frog's intestines back inside and sewed him up. Next, she took him to the creek branch that ran by our house and placed him in the water. She moved him around until he woke up. Then she let him go. About a year later she saw a frog and picked him up. Sure enough, it was the same little guy, scars and all.

I am convinced that Momma could have been a veterinarian if she had taken a different crossroad, and if she had had the money or encouragement for further education. But she chose a different path. I am grateful, for that path gave me a lifetime of love and caring that molded me into who I am today.

It is amazing how the love and support of someone you love and admire can change your life. My grandmother, Sam, (born Sallie Ann Carver before she married and became Sallie Ann Powell) was just such a person. She had so much faith and patience. She believed in the literal interpretation of the Bible and always said, "If we have faith to believe, even as small as a grain of mustard seed, and say to the mountain, 'move,' it will move."

I was witness to her faith, and to many of her answered prayers. And, I was inspired by her work ethic and love of family. Through her eyes, I learned how faith is sometimes the only thing you can hold on to when you have lost everything else that is tangible. My grandmother and I used to sit together and rock in an old porch swing. She told me endless stories about going to church, and about the times her prayers were answered. My grandmother's philosophy has saved my life on more than one occasion, but that is a story for later on.

We are a product of our environment. I had loving sets of parents and grandparents, but even though I treasured my childhood as I was living it, I never knew how good those days were until I was grown and had moved away.

Growing up in a small town is very different than life in a big city. When you grow up poor in a small town, it is the only world you know. It isolates you from many of the experiences other people take for granted. Ours was a quiet life filled with hard work, storytelling, singing hymns around the kitchen table, and going to church every time the doors were open.

We seldom left the yard except to catch the school bus, so any outing was one we looked forward to with amazement. Playtime with Shelby was playing in a gulley on a red clay dirt hillside where we spent hours building roads and cities out of rocks and sticks and tree limbs. We spent many hot summer days driving little toy trucks and cars along those roads. Shelby was my other hero. He was my big brother and I loved him more than anyone else in the whole world. I wanted to be just like him.

In addition to building roads, in the summer we played baseball and played with neighborhood kids. Sometimes, Shelby took me hunting. I recall one hunting trip when I yelled for the rabbit to run away. That ended my hunting excursions with my big brother.

On most Sunday afternoons we visited Mr. and Mrs. Davis's house (that's what I called Daddy's parents). As I mentioned before, their given names were Edward and Tilley. When Shelby and I weren't getting into something else, we played baseball in the field across from my grandparent's house. All of my cousins were boys, and none of them wanted a five-year-old girl on their team, so Sundays weren't always so special for me.

However, I do remember one Sunday that was different from the rest. Daddy was a great baseball player. Both teams always argued to see which side he would play for. Being Daddy's shadow, I begged to play and Daddy told me that I could. When we got there though, everyone else said I had to leave. Of course, I began to cry. But Daddy made everything okay when he explained that if I couldn't play, then he wouldn't play either, and he started back to the house. At that, my cousins all screamed "she can stay."

So the game began. Being five, it didn't take me long to get hot, and decide they could have their baseball game. I easily found other things to do. I have looked back on that afternoon many times and wondered why Daddy did what he did. One thing I do know is that I'll never forget the fact that he did. He made me feel like I counted to him, even if I was a girl, but, that's what daddies are supposed to do.

One of the few luxuries we had was the occasional trip to Bowling Green, Kentucky to Beech Bend Amusement Park. Momma and Daddy loved the drag races there. They especially looked forward to a special stunt car driver name Joey Chitwood, who performed occasionally in our area. One summer, Daddy took us to see Chitwood perform his stunts at the drag races. Even though it was only twenty-five miles away, it seemed like it took an eternity to get there. I remember the searing heat and unusual smells as we left the parking lot for the seating area. The park also had animals in cages and carnival rides. As a kid, it seemed like the most exciting place on earth.

I look back now, and realize that we never, ever took a vacation. As a matter of fact, I was a grown woman with a child of my own before that word ever became part of my vocabulary. Those few excursions to Beech Bend Park, a couple of Sunday afternoon swims in the creek, and a few times to the Allen County Fair were all I remember of entertainment. While I had a great early childhood, it is interesting to look back and see that I hold only a few memories of it as being extra special.

One memory that became burned into my mind happened on one of those rare Sunday outings to the drag races. I have always loved pretty things—especially clothes with lace and chiffon. Unlike today, where kids wear shorts and t-shirts, in the fifties and sixties people dressed up a bit when they went on an outing. That Sunday, Momma dressed me up in a new white nylon dress with little pink ribbons running through it. Boy, did I think I was special that day. I had on little white shoes and socks with lace on the top edges. The night before, Momma had curled my hair with bobby pins. I was all of eight years old.

After we arrived, I remember Daddy's arms around me as he held me up so I could see above the crowd. It was a hot, muggy summer day, and the stands were crowded with people pushing and straining to see the race. I was having a great time, until Momma noticed something wrong with the skirt of my dress. She began to brush her hand against it to see if it was dirt, but it wasn't. Someone in the stands next to us was smoking, and cigarette ashes had blown onto my dress and burned a huge hole in it. Needless to say, the good times were over for that day for me, and for the rest of my family because I cried all the way home.

• • •

Burned dress at the fair aside, by the time I was eight life had solidified for me and I was a very happy little girl. Then Momma told us she was having a baby. I wasn't quite sure if I liked that idea or not. After all, *I* was the baby in the family. After taking a few months to think about it, I decided it was okay and looked forward to the day when my new sibling would arrive.

Shortly before the new baby was born, my brother and I both came down with chicken pox. We were stuck in bed for a week and to help Momma, our grandmother, Sam, looked after us. We squabbled and fought as kids do, while scratching furiously with every other word.

In an effort to occupy our thoughts, Sam sternly told me to sit still and write a story. She wanted me to get my mind off my pox so I would stop scratching. My story was about Chip and Dale, two cartoon chipmunks who were popular in the fifties and sixties. When I read my words back to her, Sam made me feel as if I had written something worthy of the Pulitzer Prize. She bragged on me and told me how great it was, then asked if she could keep it. Delighted, I told her she could. I didn't realize that grandmothers do this on occasion. I just trusted her to tell me "the truth according to Sam" and believed whatever she said must be the gospel truth.

Writing those stories became my special escape in the world. Some twenty-five years later, when my grandmother died of breast cancer, I was going through an old trunk of hers and found my Chip and Dale story. I had no idea she had kept it, along with so many other poems and prayers I wrote after that morning.

When my sister Sherlene finally arrived on Halloween, I wrote about that, too. It was interesting to have a baby in the house. I had no idea babies were so loud or so messy, or that they required so much care. I wish now I could find those particular stories. Throughout my childhood I kept a journal and to my stories, I added my prayers and my conversations with God, some poetry, and later just my feelings. It became a fall back means of expression, and I found I could express on paper all the things I could never say to someone I was speaking with.

As a child who was not yet ten, I scared my mom a lot. I talked to God as if he was my best friend and playmate, and I played with angels He sent to comfort me. It is strange for some to believe, but I never knew a time when I did not believe in God or failed to feel his presence beside me. Sam's faith and encouragement also gave me a reason to believe I could make a difference in the world. I just had to have faith and believe in me as much as Sam and God did. Momma worried about her little girl, who was mature beyond her years. But Sam always said I would be just fine, and I believed her.

One thing Sam taught us was to work, and she did that by her own example. We were never so sick that she didn't say, "Get up and you will feel better. You can't lie around and expect to get well." She was tough, and she expected us to be as well.

When my grandfather developed tuberculosis, it was she who plowed the fields with an old push plow and planted a garden and tobacco. It was she who mowed the yard, cooked the meals, carried water from the branch to wash clothes in a wringer washing machine, and took in laundry and ironing to make extra money. Through all of it, she never complained.

She did say once when we were dipping water from the branch that ran by her house that "she wished I had been a little boy." She said that because she, apparently, had always wanted to be a man. Somewhere deep inside, I felt a deep-seated agony. As a little girl, I interpreted her words to mean she would have loved me better if I had been a boy. As a result, I felt less important because I was a girl. Those words made me fight harder to find my place in the world.

When I asked Momma about it, she said Sam had said that to her, too, when she was growing up. She told me that Sam loved me, and that I shouldn't let that remark stick in my mind. Although I knew deep down that she could not have loved me more than she did, her remark caused me to question my gender and purpose in life.

I now think Sam felt that if she had to work like a man, she should have been a man. It would have made her life a lot easier, and there would have been more opportunities for her. She simply had to carry too much of the load. It would be a number of years before I understood the full meaning of her statement.

Summers with Sam were full of fun and games. I might be playing outside making mud pies, and she'd yell through the screened in kitchen window to "come here for a moment." My brother Shelby and I would come loping through the yard to see what she wanted, only to be dashed with a dipper of ice cold water through the screened kitchen window. We'd then hear her howl with laughter.

One summer she didn't grow tobacco in the usual spot next to her house. Shelby and I asked if we could build a racetrack so we could get go-carts and race them. Sam never once asked where we thought a go-cart would come from. She just told us to go ahead with our plan. We spent that suffocating hot summer building a track. We worked at it from the time we got up until the time we went to bed. Sam's son, our uncle Junior, often stopped by for lunch on weekdays to watch us toil over our new dirt track.

Finally, when summer was almost over and it was time to head back to school, we were playing outside late one afternoon. We heard a noise from the church just a few yards away from our track. The noise sounded a bit like a lawn mower, but when we looked, we saw a go-cart flying down the road toward Sam's house. Shelby and I squealed and jumped up and down as the go-cart approached.

Uncle Junior had watched as we worked and sweated to build that track. Although he was a Baptist minister on Sunday, during the week he ran a body shop that rebuilt wrecked cars. He built us that go cart with steel, odd parts, and a lawn mower engine. The summer ended on such a high note. We built the track and that go cart came—just like in the movie. We had the faith and the dream, and Uncle Junior had means to make it happen.

Another time, Uncle Junior brought us used bicycles that he had refurbished in his shop. Looking back, I realize it should have been my dad doing all those things, but Dad was seldom home. It seems that Uncle Junior was a stand in when it came to things like that, and he gave our family some of our best memories. He also took us with him to church when he was preaching at revival meetings in the area.

As you might have imagined, when we were growing up we had few material things. We were taught that the scriptures were the gospel, and that every choice we made in life needed to be made based on the teaching of the scriptures. I believe that to this day. My upbringing was never preachy or judgmental. Instead, it was filled with a great deal of love and compassion. God was presented to us as a father who loves his children, even if they stray.

My grandfather, Baxter Powell, Sr., was a Baptist minister for more than fifty years when his failing health from tuberculosis cost him his life in 1966. Baw, as we called him, was born in 1892, and his father died when he was only eight years old. At that time, all children had to pitch in and work to make ends meet, so he had to miss school so that he could help the family.

In the evening, by the light of an old oil lamp, his mother taught him to read from the Bible. It was the only textbook he ever had. It was here that he found answers to the problems of the world and found a way to teach his children and grandchildren about the loving God he had found. Baw had such a thirst for knowledge.

While it aggravated me at the time, I recall coming in from school and having him insist we sit down and tell him what new word we had learned that day. We'd tell him some word and he'd grab his Webster's Dictionary to look it up so he could find out both the meaning and the spelling. Baw would have given anything for the chance to learn in a classroom, but God knew that his experiences outside of school would allow him to teach us important life lessons that a classroom could never teach.

CHAPTER 3

Foundations

Such were the foundations of my life from the time I was born until I turned twelve years old. It was here that I came to a crossroad with no idea which turn to take or where the road would lead. In Kentucky, a lot of people talk about the county they were born in. I was born and lived in Allen County, and the county next to us was Barren County. The Barren River often flooded both counties when torrential rains caused the river to rise outside its banks. The state decided the only recourse was to build a dam that would provide recreation, and curtail the periodic flooding in that region. Since my dad was logger, he got a job with the Corps of Engineers clearing timber in preparation for the new dam. Because of his experience, he was made crew foreman.

It was the summer of 1964 when Daddy started that job. Momma said that soon after, Daddy's language and demeanor changed. She thought he was running with a rough crowd and that the men he worked with were having a bad influence on him. At home, he began to tell off color jokes, something he had never done before. That summer, Robert Shelby Davis became a different man.

That same year, Daddy turned forty. I'll never know if it was a middle age crisis or the need to run from something in his past (or his present), but the man I thought hung the moon, became a man I did not know and could not understand. Years later, while the pain of Daddy's change has never gone away, Shelby and I can now joke that Daddy turned forty and turned on.

In 1964, however, Daddy apparently no longer wanted the love of a wife, or the adoration of three children, and he began to spend nights away from home. When Shelby and I ran into him on the square in town, in Scottsville, he'd cross the street and pretend he didn't know we were his kids. It was as if someone might see him talking to us and realize he was married with children. We didn't know how very close to the truth that really was—until later on.

Sometimes when Daddy came home late at night, I heard Momma ask if he had been drinking. His words always the same, "you know I don't drink." But, he stayed out later and later, and some nights did not return home at all. When he did return, he offered no excuses as to where he had been and my parents argued about it.

The three of us were very puzzled about what was happening to our simple life, and to the man we all adored and looked up to. There were too many questions, absolutely no answers, and we began to feel our family tear apart.

Sherlene turned four that year and began to suffer nervous spells from the arguing and the desperation our family shared. We all felt it, but she was way too young to deal with it. She often sat in the corner crying, and shaking uncontrollably. Summer and fall came and went, and at some point snow began to fall. As dark as that summer had been, the barren tree branches and chill in the air only made the feeling of desperation even worse. The chill of winter was approaching. Then Christmas arrived.

For some reason, when I was growing up there are blanks spots in my memory. One of these areas is Christmas. Specifically, I don't remember very many Christmas's or presents along the way. I do remember getting coloring books and crayons one year. Another year, I got a Bible and a yellow terrycloth housecoat that had a huge peacock on the back of it. I must have been all of six years old. Daddy had bought it on the roadside near Elizabethtown, Kentucky when he was on a timber run. I thought it was the most beautiful thing I had ever seen.

My most memorable Christmas, however, was in 1964. It was Christmas Eve. Momma spent the day baking pies and preparing for our traditional Christmas meal. Snow had fallen all day until the ground was covered with ten inches of white, glistening magic. It had been a quiet afternoon for Shelby, Sherlene, and me, playing inside the house. And, it remained quiet until Daddy got home. Late in the afternoon, about four o'clock, we heard a car pull into the drive. We looked out and noticed it was a taxi. That was very unusual for us. No one ever came to our house in a taxi.

We next heard the crunch of snow beneath Daddy's feet as he lumbered toward the house. That Christmas Eve was the first time I had ever seen an intoxicated man—and this one happened to be my dad. From that Christmas Eve on, our life was never the same.

That Christmas Eve afternoon, Shelby (who was soon to be fourteen), Sherlene, (who had just turned four), and I (age twelve) were sitting in the living room when the door burst open and in staggered my father. At the time, I didn't know he was drunk. I thought he was sick. But he began cursing us, and pushing Momma around. He was mean spirited and angry, and his eyes were red. He looked like the devil had spit him out of Hell itself.

My brother left the house in tears to seek refuge with my grandmother, who lived just down the hill from our house. My sister cowered in the corner, crying her heart out, while I was ordered to "fix me something to eat." I scrambled eggs, made Daddy a sandwich and set it on the table. Then my daddy grabbed the sandwich, wadded it up, and threw it in the floor as he screamed, "I'm not eating this slop."

I was so angry I was shaking. But before I could say anything, Daddy said he was burning up and threw open the back door. I watched him stumble down the back steps and fall into the snow. The snow continued to fall innocently in huge flakes. Other than the image of my dad lying there, it was beautiful outside. I felt the chill of those lovely flakes against my skin, and the heat of my tears as they ran down my face. Whatever dreams we had left of family shattered like glass. I was humiliated, horrified, and changed forever, and there wasn't anything merry about that Christmas, or any that followed, for many years. The Daddy I knew left our life that Christmas Eve, and the new version moved in and took his place.

• • •

For the next three years, our nights were filled with real life nightmares. Daddy regularly came home in a drugged and drunken haze declaring all the ways he would kill us. Many nights, I took knives and guns away from him. My brother and I took turns going to church so that Momma wouldn't be caught alone with Daddy. He made many attempts to kill her, so one of us had to stay behind to watch after her. Once, he tried to strangle her. Another time he threw a knife at her that lodged in the wall next to her chair. He also punched dozens of holes in the walls with his fists.

As much as Daddy tortured Momma, he never struck me with anything but words. But those words cut deeper than any knife. They bruised my soul more than fists or rocks ever could have. Night after night my mother prayed that he would change, and return to us as he was before. As the bills began to pile up and creditors knocked at the door, Momma made the decision to get a job. She had to. There was no food and the electricity was about to be turned off. She interviewed, and was offered the same job twice. Both times, Daddy found out and destroyed her paperwork, saying, "no wife of his was going to work."

Daddy was so jealous. Many times he accused her of having someone in the house, just because he saw tire tracks in the driveway. The only tracks were from bill collectors who came to take away our furniture. They appeared several times, saying she had co-signed on loans. But Momma knew she hadn't co-signed anything. She told them to "get," before she called the law for letting someone forge her name. Armed with Shelby's pellet gun, she chased the bill collectors away from the house.

Momma continued to look for work and finally secured a job at Washington Overall Manufacturing Company. She started by seaming pants, but worked her way up to an inspector on the line. My grandmother fed us and loved us when Momma was at work. It was now two grown women and three kids against the world.

After our "special" Christmas Eve, Momma started sleeping in the bed with my sister and me. There were countless nights when Daddy came home during the night and pulled Mom out of the bed cursing, and swearing he would kill her. The fights went on for hours. We would end up getting just a few hours sleep before heading off to school. Shelby and I never told anyone at school what our new life was like, in fear that students and teachers alike might look down their noses at us.

One particular night was worse than the others. A few days before, a man in Scottsville had killed his wife and kids. Apparently, this presented my father with the idea of a way to rid himself of the responsibilities of his family. Eventually, we all came to a crossroad. This time the choice was to live or die. My entire family was standing on the threshold of eternity.

That dark evening, around midnight, we heard the taxi's tire crush the gravel in the driveway. We woke up and began to prepare ourselves for what was heading our way, but this time, nothing we did could have prepared us. Daddy staggered in with a pistol in his hand. He told us he intended to kill us all and burn the house down before killing himself. He said he would also set fire to my grandparent's house and when they began to run out, he'd shoot them in the head and watch their eyes pop out.

Daddy dragged our momma out of my bed and into their bedroom. He then sat on the foot of their bed and rolled the cylinder of the gun he carried. He said that he would not sleep until he had ended all of our lives. By this time Daddy was a wild man with red, bloodshot eyes that stared out of a face I barely recognized. Daddy pointed the pistol at Momma's head while she sat huddled on the floor praying, rocking back and forth. I was in the next room on my bed praying, begging God to not let him do what he had come home to do. As I prayed, I wrote the words down in my journal.

I heard Daddy yell, "No one can get to you tonight. Your lives are mine to take into eternity and into Hell with me." I knew Daddy meant every word he was saying. But, I also knew that God was with us. God was way bigger than Daddy. I prayed even harder that God would end this night safely for us all. Sherlene, who was six, sobbed in the bed beside me, and my brother was quiet in the next room.

Over and over Daddy repeated the words that no one could stop him. No one could save us from him. My mother cried, and rocked back and forth as she prayed. All at once Momma sat up straight. I felt a rush of calm pour over me and I felt the power of God in the room as she began to speak, "There *is* someone who can get to you, Bob. He is here now."

Momma mocked Daddy, as strength filled her veins and mine. He cursed her again and denied that anyone could reach him, that he had no intention of sleeping until we were all dead. But suddenly, he grew quiet. It was as if someone had turned off a light switch. I watched through the door in amazement as Daddy suddenly fell back across the foot of the bed, asleep.

I scrambled out of my bed and into the room where he lay. Shelby joined Momma and me as I pried the pistol from his fingers. Then Shelby and I took the gun outside and buried it under a pine tree where Daddy couldn't find it. By this time Momma had gathered up Sherlene and joined us outside. We had stood on the threshold of death and God had sent his angels to save us. The hours of agony and threats were over.

When we gathered outside on the front steps of our house, my grandmother, Sam, was waiting at the door. Sam had heard everything that had happened inside. She too, had felt God's power and knew the worst was over. Dawn started to break and the horizon began to turn red. It had been five hours of madness but we had survived. Sam stood there ashen faced and said, "I have always heard that the darkest hours are just before the dawn. I think tonight we have seen the true meaning of those words."

Momma always said that when God answers a prayer, He answers a prayer. She was never afraid of Daddy after that night. After that evening, Daddy never threatened to kill us again. He continued to torture us with his drinking, cussing, and verbal abuse. But even with all the torture that Daddy heaped on her, Momma believed she could not divorce him without the scriptural evidence of adultery.

All she had at this point was suspicion. She asked people she worked with, but no one would admit they knew anything. She kept asking, though, and waited for the day when she would have the proof. One Saturday morning Momma loaded up the car with all of us and headed into town to drive down a street where she suspected Daddy was staying with a woman. As we started down the street, we met a car that was heading toward us. We could all see that Daddy was in it, and with him was his new woman. He was caught.

That day was freedom day for us—or at least a beginning. Momma filed for divorce the next Monday morning, and the judge told her that my father could be ordered to pay child support and alimony. She declined both. She didn't want anything from him but her freedom. Momma knew he wouldn't pay anyway, and why let the courts meddle with our lives? Momma's position was that a man doesn't owe you because he once loved you. Why would she want something from someone who no longer cared?

Momma had so much faith, that somehow we managed to survive very tough times with no help from my father. We never had any government help. We never had help from the church. Momma was way too private and far too proud to ask for anything. Perhaps that is why I have always had such a hard time asking for help.

During the years when Momma was working at the factory, and later with her second job waiting tables, I worried about her. She worked so hard and stood on concrete floors eight hours a day, barely earning enough money to feed and clothe us. My mother and grandmother were two of the strongest, most unselfish women I have ever known in my life. From them, I learned to be strong and to have faith in things you cannot see.

Robert and Pauline Davis, my Mom and Dad

CHAPTER 4

On My Own

When I was thirteen, I met my first boyfriend on the Allen County school bus. He was the son of Ben Shipley, who owned and ran Shipley's Country Store. Bennie Shipley played drums for the high school band, and I thought he was much quieter and far more mature than the other dimwits who rode that bus. He even wore glasses and sports coats to school. Every day I watched him get on the bus and thought he was awesome.

One rainy day, Bennie got on the school bus and sat down next to me. He asked if I had a Kleenex so he could clean the rain off his glasses. I told him I didn't, and his response shattered me. "I thought *all* girls carried Kleenexes in their purses," he said. What I heard in that sentence was that I didn't measure up.

I have since realized that I don't always interpret things the way they are intended. What is often said is not what I hear internally. Must be that Mars / Venus thing we have all heard about. I was crushed by Bennie's words. At thirteen, I was so insecure and shy. I was at that awkward time between child and woman when girls aren't quite sure where they fit. Even though I was in the eighth grade, I was already forced to wear sweaters to cover up my well-endowed chest, and now Bennie was telling me I didn't measure up. I was trembling, but thankfully we were nearing my bus stop and I quickly got off the bus.

Needless to say, my insecurities were in overload. To be different at thirteen is to stand out when all you want to do is blend in. Today, I still do not feel I am like other girls. But today, I am proud of my differences. I tend to fill up my pockets with business cards instead of lipstick. My purse won't hold everything, so I'm probably carrying a cell phone, camera, and notebook but have still probably forgot the Kleenex. And you know what? I am okay with that.

Little did I know, but that young man on the school bus was the man I would marry three short years later, during the summer between my sophomore and junior year of high school. After that initial school bus conversation, I figured I would never be noticed by Bennie Shipley again. I was wrong. On the last day of my eighth grade school year, the only theater in Scottsville was running a new John Wayne movie, *Donovan's Reef.* Several of us from school had walked to town to watch the film.

The movie was just about to start when Bennie Shipley leaned over and asked if he could sit next to me. I said yes, but before he could sit down, another boy jumped into the seat and began to sing, "Wild thing, I think I love you" to me. I told him that I wasn't wild and I didn't love him, so move. But it was too late. My first choice was gone and I was stuck with "Mr. Wild Thing."

About six weeks later, Bennie invited me to his sixteenth birthday party at his parents' home. I was ecstatic when Momma gave me permission to go. I didn't know many of the kids at the party but I was really only interested in Bennie. In the middle of the party Bennie asked me to walk outside with him, and we began to walk through the yard and around the house. There under a hot July full-moon sky, he kissed me. It was my first kiss, and I really did feel the earth move under my feet. I was still just thirteen years old, and couldn't believe this smart young man was interested in me.

That night began a three-year dating period that resulted in our marriage. Momma cautioned me about moving quickly, and said I was too young to be thinking about marriage. But I thought about it anyway. A lot.

One afternoon when I was fifteen Momma was standing in the garden when I ran out to her, sporting an engagement ring.

"I love him and want to get married," I said.

"The things you love about him now," she wisely replied, "will dim with time, and the things you don't like about him now will only grow larger. You need to give it more time."

Bennie and I planned to wait to get married until I graduated in 1971, but when you are fifteen, days seem like years. When my brother ran off and got married to his high school sweetheart the next year, it pushed Bennie and me to make our nuptials sooner than planned.

Like all little girls, I dreamed of a church wedding full of flowers and a long white dress and veil. When we began to plan the ceremony, Bennie's mother, Annie Mae, began talking about all the people they needed to invite. I quickly realized that my mother couldn't afford a fancy wedding. She certainly couldn't afford to pay for a reception. Furthermore, I would never ask Momma to do it, so the big church wedding was off.

I never mentioned those dreams to her. I knew I couldn't have a store bought dress, so Momma made me a white dotted-Swiss, knee length gown. She took a piece of lace and made a bow for my hair and that had to do. The church wedding would have to be a dream for someone else. I was thrilled when Uncle Junior agreed to marry us. We were married in his old turn of the century two-story house, and our reception was at Bennie's sister's home a few miles away.

Bennie and I honeymooned in Cumberland Falls, Kentucky. We certainly couldn't afford a trip to Niagara Falls, so we decided to make it to Corbin, Kentucky and see the falls there. It was under a three-hour drive, and we could drive there by night fall. Years later, I finally made it to Niagara Falls, and I can assure you that while Cumberland Falls is beautiful, it cannot compare to the larger falls on our country's Canadian border.

For the first six months of our marriage, Bennie and I lived with Annie Mae and Ben Shipley, Bennie's parents. We slept on the sofa bed in the front living room of their house. In addition to going to school, I kept house for everyone and cooked meals.

In the morning I got up and caught the six A.M. bus to school with Bennie's father. He drove the school bus in the morning before he opened up the store. A lot of girls in my town quit school when they got married, and many married because they were pregnant. That was not the case with me. I loved school and it never occurred to me to walk away from it. I was an honor student and a class officer. I felt no inclination to walk away from that no matter how hard it was to juggle class, being a wife, and working a full time job. Staying in school was one of the best decisions I ever made.

• • •

The summer before we married Bennie had been hired at WCDS, a small AM radio station in the neighboring town of Glasgow. For several years he made the thirty-mile drive every day. Later, I often went to the station to visit Bennie when he was on the air in Scottsville, Kentucky at WLVK, especially after Shelby also got a job as a DJ at the same station. At night, Bennie talked to me about his dreams of working at a large market radio station. He had Nashville in his sights and that scared me more than I wanted to admit. Somehow, I just couldn't see me raising a family in a big city like Nashville. Of course, I had never been to Nashville, even though it was less than seventy miles away. I had never even crossed the Kentucky state line.

Ten months after we married, in April 1970, Bennie was inducted into the army. The Vietnam War was raging and both of us feared that if he went overseas he might never return. Every evening Walter Cronkite read off the daily death toll and one name after the other joined the hundreds of thousands of men and women whose lives had been lost in that war. Several of Bennie's friends were sent to Vietnam and several came back home changed forever.

I cried and cried when Bennie left for boot camp. Bennie wasn't like his father. He didn't own a gun. He didn't hunt or fish. As a matter of fact, he hated the outdoors. He really was a pacifist. But Uncle Sam didn't care; he took him anyway. This was a time when young men were drafted regardless of their feelings about the military. Some people are simply not cut out for that life. Their talents are better used elsewhere.

Bennie was in basic training for less than ninety days when he contracted the flu and an inner ear infection that created a nervous disorder that would plague his life and our marriage for years to come. The strong, loving, young man, who left for the Army in April, was not the one who returned to me in July.

While Bennie was in boot camp, I worked from three until nine every evening and on Saturdays at Gibson's Discount Center, an upscale version of the Dollar General stores owned by the same

Turner family. I actually worked thirty-six hours a week and attended school full time during my last two years of high school.

At work and at school, I counted the days until I could see my husband again. When Bennie received a medical discharge, he returned to the job he had left behind at WCDS Radio. But I soon found out that he now suffered from depression and nervousness. He was continually withdrawn and edgy. While we had been married less than a year and were mere teenagers, he no longer wanted me to touch him, and he pulled away from me whenever I tried.

The passionate nineteen-year-old who went into the army had lost interest in me by the time he returned. I couldn't understand what had changed. Little did I know that he was taking a prescription for Valium, which was complicating his problem. Unbeknownst to me, Bennie had gone to a local doctor who had prescribed the medication for his nerves.

I am sure that my own insecurities added to the mix. I tried so hard to be a good wife and suddenly I felt rejection. I internalized my fear and wondered what I had done to drive him away. I also asked myself how I could pull him back to me. I look back on it now and realize I was too young and too inexperienced to understand what was happening. Ultimately, everything combined to increase the problem and the stress on the two of us.

One night when I was at work, I got a call from Bennie's boss at the radio station. He wanted to know where Bennie was.

"Why are you calling me?" I asked. "Wasn't he at work today? He left for work this morning."

"I haven't seen him in a week," his boss replied.

Bennie had left the house each morning as if he was going to work. But as soon as I left for school, Bennie came back home. When I got home that evening, we had a huge fight. I flushed his Valium down the commode and told him to get a grip. Bennie apologized. He promised to stop taking the medication and return to work. Several weeks later, however, I found a new vial of pills in the glove compartment of his '68 Camaro. That did it for me. I lost all trust in him, but I had no idea that our problems were just beginning.

Our troubles continued as I neared my high school graduation. As a graduation present, my mother deeded me a small lot next to her house. Bennie and I then began to look for a mobile home to place on it. I was hopeful that the house would be one solution to our problems. We drove over twenty miles to Bowling Green, Kentucky in search of a small mobile home that we could afford, and we found one. It was a ten-foot by fifty-four-foot, two bedroom, one bath, piece of heaven. We gladly paid out seventy-five dollars a month for a home we could call our own.

I could barely believe that we were out of the in-laws house and into our very own place! We watched as the truck pulled it into the driveway and began to set it on cement blocks. Moving day was so exciting, and I was sure that life was now going to get much, much better.

• • •

At Gibson's Discount Center I worked in the basement sporting goods department stocking oil, paint, guns, and ammunition. Because I was still in school, I worked the closing shift and on Saturdays. One night, about thirty minutes before we closed, a man came in and asked to see a 12-gauge shotgun. I opened the gate and went behind the counter to pull down the gun he requested. When I handed it to him, he looked down the barrel of the gun, and asked, "How do you know it's a 12-gauge?"

"It's written on the side of the barrel and on the price tag," I said

"Let's see," he replied.

He proceeded to pull two 12-gauge shells from his pocket, popped them into the chamber and pointed the gun directly at me. I was stunned. For what seemed like an eternity, I looked down the barrel of that loaded 12-gauge shotgun and into the eyes of a stranger whose intentions I did not know. Was this a robbery, or did he have other motives in mind? Was this to be my last breath?

The man finally broke his stare with me and said, "I guess you're right."

He broke down the gun, popped out the shells, turned, and headed for the exit. I looked around, but there were no other personnel on that floor. Any shouts from me would not be heard upstairs. Shaking, I raced to the phone to call my manager, who was at the front check out, but the man had already vacated the building.

I always wondered what the man's intentions were that night, and why he didn't pull the trigger. What did he see in my eyes that caused him to turn and walk away? Had he made a different decision at that crossroad in his life, this story would have ended before it began.

• • •

During my early married years, I dreamed many dreams. Most of them were simple dreams about writing books and doing something with my life. I wanted to go to college. I wrote notebooks full of poetry, prose, and prayers. I spilled my guts and my soul into those pages, capturing the pain that I felt through my childhood.

I graduated Allen County High School in three and a half years. I was an honor student and an officer of several school clubs. Because I graduated early, I left school in December to work full time, but I attended graduation in May 1971 with my other classmates. Even though I graduated with honors, I didn't know how to apply for college, or anything about financial assistance. I didn't even know anyone who had been to college.

Unfortunately, my teachers and counselors never bothered to explain how college functioned. I didn't know there were grants for children who could not afford to go. My high school teachers failed to push me toward a collegiate goal even though I was an honor student. Because I got married at sixteen, my teachers apparently believed I would never try to be anything more than a housewife or a store clerk.

As I said before, most girls who marry at sixteen do so because they are expecting a child, but I was not pregnant. When three years passed and there were still no children, people finally figured out that it was simply a marriage of two young people in love. Part of my decision to marry young was because it allowed my mother to have one less mouth to feed. In this way, I could make it in the world and not be a burden to her.

Plus, Bennie was two years older than I was and money earned from his job paid for my high school books. He also showed me in many other ways that he cared. I had never known that kind of love and support from a man. Bennie allowed me to believe in romance, and showed me that a man could express love and tenderness. He was so very different from my father. Bennie encouraged me, and believed without a doubt that I could accomplish anything I set my mind to.

Like my grandmother, Bennie encouraged me to dream big. He had big dreams for himself, but he also helped me dream my own dreams. Sam supported me the same way. Throughout high school I always believed I would go to college. I took all the preparatory classes, but college initially eluded me. It would be several years before I finally got my chance to experience it first hand.

When I graduated in 1971, I continued to work full time earning $1.50 per hour. Whenever there was a holiday, I got time and half and accepted overtime anytime it was available. I was nineteen, and married for three years, when I became pregnant with our only child, Michael. The college life I dreamed of had not come true for me, and I had not experienced growing up like others kids. I did not experience school trips in high school, college dorms, dating, or living on my own. I was an old, old soul, and I wasn't even twenty. All I knew was hard work and responsibility. But, the challenges I faced in my early life helped me become a strong woman who was able to deal with the many circumstances that would churn throughout my life. I am one of the most blessed individuals you will ever know.

The first five years of marriage were a financial struggle. I also had never been to a doctor before—and certainly not for something as private as a pregnancy. For a long time, I did not tell anyone what I suspected. Finally, I made an appointment where my suspicions were confirmed. The doctor told me I could expect a baby around the end of August.

A few weeks after that appointment, I felt the baby move for the first time. I was terrified, and re-read the materials the doctor gave me. One part of me was ready to be a mom but another part was struggling, resisting. There was so much I wanted to do that I felt unprepared to take on this new responsibility. To add to my stress, Momma wouldn't discuss anything about my pregnancy. As close as we are now, I did not feel then that I could speak to her about the changes going on in my body. Most of my other friends were in college, so I couldn't ask them. Besides, they had not experienced what I was going through. So, I read a few books and figured it out alone.

One day late in June, a salesman stopped by our house trying to sell us smoke detectors. Because I was very pregnant, he used it as a means of scaring me into buying the alarms. He began to paint a picture of my baby smothering in a crib, and if I cared about my child I'd make sure we had enough alarms to indicate fire. The man specifically spoke of mobile home fires and how quickly they spread. By the time he left I was hysterical. I walked the yard in tears and couldn't shake the sadness I was feeling. About nine-thirty that evening, I began to feel incredible pain as my labor began. It was only June 27th and the doctor indicated the baby's due date as the end of August. Could I be that early? Would my baby survive?

Bennie grabbed my bags and we jumped into his 1968 Camaro and headed to T. J. Samson Community Hospital in Glasgow, Kentucky, some twenty-five miles away. As would be the case, my own doctor was on vacation so another doctor in his practice became responsible for the delivery. Shortly after I arrived—and all through the night—an Amazon of a nurse came into my room to check my progress. I swear, her hands were the size of catcher's mitts. Each exam was more painful than the last. At one point I remember turning to Bennie and telling him if he ever "did that" to me again I would kill him. Pain certainly makes us say cruel things. Around ten the next morning I finally asked the nurse if there was anything she could give me for pain.

"Sure, honey," she said. "You just have to ask for it."

About ninety minutes later at 11:56 A.M., Bennie Michael Shipley was born. I had my son by natural childbirth, without the breathing lessons we all see in the movies. He weighed seven pounds, eleven ounces, and had a head full of dark hair and the prettiest dark brown eyes I had ever seen. Apparently the doctor had miscalculated. I definitely had a full term baby boy.

Bennie and I brought Michael home and began life as parents. Momma and Sam were the doting grandparent and great-grandparent, and guided me through the many questions I had. I felt more comfortable asking them about my baby than I had my body. Several times, I walked next door to get Momma to help me when I could not get Michael to go to sleep. Each time, as soon as she held him, he instantly stopped crying. Momma always said that a baby knows when you are tired or anxious. They can feel it in your arms.

Bennie's mom, Annie Mae Shipley worked at Dollar General and kept Michael in baby clothes. Almost every week she brought him the cutest outfits. Momma also knew someone who gave us a huge case of diapers, which helped immensely. Even thought our mortgage payment was only seventy-five dollars a month, it was a huge portion of our income in 1972. I thought about going back to work at Gibson's on a part-time basis, but the only way I could do that was if Momma watched Michael. She was only thirty-eight then and was working two jobs and dating a handsome man who had taken a fancy to her. The timing really wasn't right.

• • •

The time became right for Momma a few years later, however. But not with my child. Because of the age difference, and the fact that I married at sixteen, my sister Sherlene and I never had a chance to grow as close as most sisters do. Plus, as my sister began to grow into a little girl, I started to see distinct differences in our personality. I was the one who towed the line and played by the rules. She aggravated me by coloring in my books or messing with something of mine. Sherlene was a wild child from the beginning. If I said black, she said white. We came from the same parents, but neither our looks nor our personalities mirrored them.

When I married at sixteen, Sherlene was just eight years old. In her early teens she began to run with a wild crowd and by thirteen was pregnant with her first child, Amy, who my momma later raised. Sherlene also ran away from home on more than one occasion, which terrified my mother and grandmother. Several times I came home to get in the car with Momma and drive the back roads looking for her.

By fifteen, Sherlene was pregnant with a son who would be named James. My mother swore she would not raise a second child for her and Sherlene planned to put him up for adoption. Nearing the time of delivery, my soft-hearted Momma decided she could not see a grandchild of hers given away, so she agreed to bring him home. In addition to the three birth children Momma raised, she reared two more as her own and instilled in them the same values she instilled in us. My sister has struggled with men, drugs, and alcohol her entire life. I am quite sad to say those things have prevented us from being as close as sisters should be.

• • •

Several years passed, during which Bennie and I made ends meet, but barely. Michael had just turned two when Bennie came home from work to announce that he had been offered a job at WSM-AM, a radio station in Nashville, Tennessee. He was so excited to finally work in a large market. It was his dream—a dream he had from the time he knew what radio was. For the job offer to be from a legendary station such as WSM-AM was even more incredible.

As proud as I was for Bennie and this new opportunity, I felt my heart sink at the thought of leaving my home and everything that was comfortable to me. Now I was faced with a move to a city where there were skyscrapers and freeways and thousands of people I did not know. No family to talk to. No friends. I was more frightened than I had ever been in my life, and my insecurities and fears set in. I did not want to go, and I told him so. Bennie surprised me with his reaction.

While we had argued and had our differences, I had never questioned my love for my husband. He told me to make my choice, but he was going. He said we could get a divorce if I didn't want to go. I thought about that. I didn't want a divorce. I didn't want my child to be a child of parents who were not together and feel the shame and awkwardness I had felt. Like my mother, I believed marriage was for life.

Many days of indecision passed during which I realized that Bennie really would choose Nashville and his dream over Michael and me. One more crossroad, one more choice. Scottsville or Nashville? Would we stay together and raise our child together, or divorce? I looked into my heart and knew that marriage was for better or for worse and a wife is supposed to support her husband. So, I decided to join him. We packed a big U-Haul truck and set out for Nashville. It was August 1974.

My son, Michael when he started first grade

CHAPTER 5

Nashville, Tennessee - Music City, USA

Times were hard in 1974—at least they were for the Shipley family. Bennie's paycheck at WSM did not stretch far enough to cover the rent, groceries, and car payment. We were never late paying bills, but there was never any money left over for other necessities. We ate a lot of macaroni, Ramen noodles, beans, and cornbread. When Michael was a toddler I was able to make many of his clothes—those Bennie's mom did not bring home from work—but as he grew into a young boy, that became more difficult. Little boys need jeans and shirts once they grow out of their baby outfits.

Plus, if Bennie and I argued a lot in Kentucky, we fought even more in Nashville. The financial stress on our marriage seemed unbearable. I became selfish. I was lonely, and I thought more about the home and family I lost than the home I was trying to build in Nashville. Looking back, I know I made it harder on Bennie than it had to be. For all the struggles I had known in my childhood, I realize now that I had a lot of growing up to do. Bennie, probably fed up with my whining and depression, advised me to find a job. Yes, we needed the extra income but I think Bennie felt we needed something else in our lives if we were to survive.

"Get out of the house and meet some people," Bennie said. "I have friends through work. You need to make friends, too."

Bennie looked in the newspaper and circled jobs he thought I should apply for. I was terrified. I was the shy Kentucky girl who had never been away from home. I had little confidence, trusted no one, and fully believed that mothers should stay at home and take care of their children until they were in school. I wore guilt like it was a cloak of armor.

At that time Michael was only two and a half. If I was frightened about the move, I was terrified at what might happen to my son in another caretaker's hands. Consumed by fear that I would fail as a mother and a wife, I agreed to look for work. For the next year and a half I looked for a job and went on interviews. My weight dropped to 104 pounds. My hands cracked open and bled from a nervous rash that I developed from stress. I almost gave up hope of finding a job. Plus, when I looked at what jobs were paying, I felt it didn't make sense for me to work. It was hard to find a job that would pay enough for me to pay child care, a car (which I would need to go back and forth to work), and have anything left over to bring relief to the financial burden we were under.

At one point our family doctor told me he was looking for someone to work in his front office and offered the job to me. I worked a few days before I realized that the job was more stress than not having a paycheck. I couldn't believe the cattiness of my co-workers and their discussions about patients as they came and departed. They discussed their ailments and other confidential information they read from their charts. I quit after a few days, then interviewed at a bank and was offered a job as a bank teller. Soon after, I learned I would have to train in downtown Nashville, and my deep fear of big city skyscrapers overtook my common sense. The Friday before I was to start, I called to turn down the job.

Bennie never gave up hope for me, though. He believed in me more than I believed in myself, and suggested that I check into evening college courses. I explored that idea out and found out that because we earned so little, I could get a grant to pay for school. I enrolled at the University of Tennessee at Nashville and began taking English literature, philosophy, and journalism. I received an A+ in philosophy and my professor commented that he had never given that grade to any student in all his years of teaching. My English literature professor said my writing was better than most people who wrote for newspapers. Maybe I should try to get a job with a magazine while I worked on my degree.

I was stunned. For the first time in my adult life, a professional person had praised me for my work. When we spoke, he praised my reasoning ability and said I could accomplish any goal I set out for myself. I was in the real world and at that moment felt on top of the universe. I drove home that night from class and couldn't wait to tell Bennie what the professor had said. I knew

Bennie would be proud, and he was. Smiling, he said, "I told you so."

I tried, but every company I interviewed with wanted a degree. At the rate I was going, attending school just at night, it would take me ten years to get my degree. So, I continued to take classes while I searched for a job. My college experience, however, and the professors who encouraged me, gave me my first degree of confidence. I so appreciated Bennie's encouragement to step outside my comfort zone and go to school. It was the first step in helping me grow into the woman I am today. Without his constant prodding and pushing I might never have spread my wings, let alone attempted to fly.

Since I had been around radio people most of my adult life, I felt comfortable in radio stations. I took a radio production class in Nashville and it was there that I met a man named Cecil Thomas, who taught the course. Cecil was general manager for WMAK, one of the leading rock stations in Nashville. Cecil was bald, well dressed, and probably twenty years older than I was.

Night after night in class, he picked me out to make conversation. I was so nervous around him and couldn't figure out if he wanted to flirt with me or encourage me. Finally, one night he approached me after class and asked a question I will never forget.

"You don't like yourself, do you?" he said.

I was stunned. How dare he ask me such a question? I glared at him for a moment. Then he looked me directly in the eye and asked the same question again. Dropping my eyes to think it over, I told him he was right. I didn't like me and I felt insecure around everyone I met.

Cecil then wisely said, "Let me give you some words of advice. Learn to look at yourself as others see you, and not as you see yourself. Listen to your own conversations as if you were hearing them through someone else's ears. If you don't like something about the person you are listening to, or the actions or feelings she is feeling, change it. If you like it, keep it. One day you will be a beautiful person that the world will love, and you will see yourself as I see you now."

Cecil became a friend and confidante who continued to encourage and believe in me. He told me stories of women who worked in his sales department who exceeded all of the expectations and sales records of their male counterparts. He told me that I, too, could accomplish that—if I believed.

Cecil became a mentor to me. He encouraged me to dream big and taught me how to love myself, regardless of what I was feeling inside. For years we stayed in touch. I am lucky that a stranger became a friend and helped me grow so much in those early years in Nashville. More than anyone, he helped me overcome my insecurities.

In the late 1970s, you had to have an FCC Third Class Radio Operator's License to work in radio. I liked the idea of being in radio and on the air, so I studied and obtained my license. After my radio production class, I interviewed at 93Z FM, a local easy listening station. From everything the program director said during my interview, I believed I had the job. Easy listening stations were about the only place women could get on air in the late seventies. By now, Bennie had switched air shifts and was working for WSM-FM which was a top 40 station at that time. When the program director discovered my husband was the morning jock on WSM-FM (then a top 40 station), he retracted the job offer, saying it was a conflict of interest. I was devastated. I finally found a job I wanted and I was deprived of it because my husband worked in radio on the other side of town? But, I quickly put the rejection behind me and did as Cecil said. I began to dream bigger and before long a new dream began to take birth inside of me.

Most evenings I watched a Nashville news program, and discovered they had a TV personality named Huel Howser who did human-interest stories. I wanted to be a woman on TV who did that. I wanted to create special interest stories and touch people with what I uncovered. I applied at Channel 5 News, and to my surprise and delight, secured an interview with the general manager. It turned out that the news department required employees to have a degree in journalism before they even let you work as an intern. He asked if I had ever used a calculator. Believe it or not I hadn't, but I said I had. It was just a small white lie. He then offered me a job during the upcoming election night. Precincts would call in votes and I, along with several others, would tabulate them for the news broadcast. (This was long before the wonderful computer systems we have today.)

I took the man up on his offer and had one glorious night behind the scenes at the television station. The door to my career had cracked open. Afterward, the general manager told me there were no full-time job openings at Channel 5 but he would keep me in mind if something developed. My search for work continued.

Bennie asked some of his co-workers to keep an ear out for an entry level job opening that was appropriate for his wife. Mary Catherine Murphy, the music director for WSM, quickly told Bennie about a receptionist job at Monument Records. Monument was an independent label whose legendary artists included Dolly Parton, Kris Kristofferson, Roy Orbison, Larry Gatlin, Connie Smith, Ray Stevens, and countless other country acts. Once again, I stood at a crossroad that would change my destiny without my even knowing it. Mine changed with that first interview—and the next six interviews that followed—before I was awarded a position that changed my life in a multitude of ways.

Monument Records was founded by Fred Foster and Buddy Deane in 1958. Buddy was a prominent Washington DC disc jockey at WTTG, and Fred had worked as a salesman in various retail stores in the Washington DC area. Years earlier, Fred came across a song called "Gotta Travel On" from a young artist named Billy Grammer, and took it to several labels to see if he could get it placed. Everyone turned him down, so he borrowed a few hundred dollars from Buddy Deane and they started Monument Records, releasing "Gotta Travel On" as their first single. The song reached *Billboard's* Top 5, sold nine hundred thousand copies, and started a dance craze called "The Shag."

Buddy Deane left the company soon thereafter and Fred became the sole owner, moving its headquarters from Washington, DC to Hendersonville, Tennessee, a small suburb just north of Nashville. The signing of former Sun Records artist Roy Orbison brought more success to Monument Records, beginning with the 1960 release, "Only the Lonely."

By 1961, a company called London Records was distributing more than forty independent record companies, prompting Foster to move Monument to the independent-distributor network. But by 1971, Foster had signed a world-wide distribution agreement with CBS Records.

In addition to Orbison and the others previously mentioned, Monument became home to artists such as Robert Knight, Jeannie Seely, Boots Randolph, Cindy Walker, Tony Joe White, Charlie McCoy, Willie Nelson, Tommy Roe, The Velvets, Connie Smith, and actor Robert Mitchum. Fred also started an R&B label called Sound Stage 7 in 1963. Artists on Sound Stage 7 included Joe Simon, The Dixie Belles, Arthur Alexander, and Ivory Joe Hunter.

Needless to say, my first introduction into a Nashville record label was not typical. Fred was an entrepreneur who had an ear for talent. It didn't matter the format. Most other labels limited themselves to specific styles of music, but Fred's unique vision created one of the most successful independent label operations in America.

From the beginning of the interview process, I found that the record business is like no other. The people are different. The offices are different. Job interviews were *very* different. In 1975, Nashville's music community was made up of old-line leaders that had seen the likes of Patsy Cline and Hank Williams, Sr. develop to stardom. By the time I interviewed for a job at Monument Records, the offices had relocated to Music Row.

Music Row is an area between 16th and 18th Avenues South that runs the better part of a mile in length. It is where most of the record studios, publishing companies, and record labels housed their offices. The original Monument office building looked a bit like a southern plantation house, or maybe a funeral home. It even had a breezeway that would have been perfectly suited for an ambulance to pull up and collect a body.

A phone call was made and I secured an appointment for my first music business interview. I was anxious, and not quite sure what to expect. I entered the double front doors of Monument into a lobby of black and white marble floors and a grand stairway to the left that led up to the offices of Fred Foster and his support staff. Gold and platinum awards lined the walls of the lobby and the long corridors on either side. Knees a bit wobbly, I informed the young woman at the desk that I had a job interview.

I had been informed that they were interviewing for the receptionist position. When I was ushered back into one of the offices, I was informed that another position had just become available and that was the job I was interviewing for. My interview was with Frank Dileo who headed up Monument's pop promotion labels. Frank had worked for Columbia Records in New York before taking on the leadership role for Monument. He was a mover and shaker, and a very fast talker. Frank was looking for a secretary. I didn't know a whole lot about being a secretary but I was willing to learn.

One of the biggest eye openers I had that day was the amount of profanity that was tossed out. As I sat in his office, he took several phone calls and utilized the "f-word" as a noun, verb, and adjective. He explained that he talked that way and might direct it at me sometimes whether I deserved it or not.

"If that happened," he asked, "how would you react?"

"If you directed it at me, it had better be for a good reason and not because you were having a bad day," I replied.

He laughed and I figured I had failed his test. At the end of the interview he said he'd let me know. I left his office wondering if this was what the music business was all about. If so, I wasn't sure it was the place for me. Needless to say, I did not get that job at Monument the first time I interviewed, nor the second or third or fourth or fifth. But I did learn a lot about men's opinions about a woman's place, and my future looked bleak. When Dileo left Monument a few months after my interview, it was to become the manager for a dynamic young singer named Michael Jackson.

About a year later, Mary Catherine Murphy once again informed Bennie that a job at Monument was available. You guessed it. They were looking for a receptionist. I called and set up another interview. This time, I was ushered into the office of Rick Blackburn, who was the vice president and general manager. When I arrived that morning, busy secretaries named Bettye and Beth made their bosses coffee and set appointments. Neither of the women seemed to have last names. At least, I never heard any. Their identities did not seem to matter in the big scheme of things. The women were just there to serve, and their contributions were not recognized. This was a time of "old-line leadership" where leaders opinions counted and followers opinions did not.

Bettye came out to greet me and ushered me into Rick's office where I was asked to sit in a chair in front of Rick's massive cherry desk. Behind him was a wall full of gold records and awards of recognition. I sat in awe of this man whose contribution had been so great.

After studying my resume, Rick looked up and said, "I noticed that you have no short hand skills."

Since I was interviewing for a receptionist job, I asked why such skills would be important.

"The label believes in promoting from within, and someday if you work hard, you might be promoted to being secretary to the president," he said. "Being the president's secretary would require short hand. So, by having that skill, you would have more opportunity for advancement."

Something inside me burned. Somewhere deep inside me a light ignited. I could not believe what I had just heard. Now, while my only job experience had been working as a sales clerk at Gibson's, I felt that Rick's words limited my intelligence. Did he think I wanted to be a receptionist forever? I hated television shows that downplayed women's roles and made secretaries look like they were a level below human. At that moment, all that frustration boiled to the surface. I opened my mouth and asked the question that probably cost me the job, "Am I to understand that if I work hard and prove myself worthy, there is no way I can become a manager of a department?"

His response was cool and to the point, "Absolutely not," he retorted, "There is no way you can move from a secretarial position to a management level position at this or any other label."

You guessed it. I didn't get the job.

By now, we had been in Nashville about eighteen months. Michael was about four and we had moved from our first apartment on Charlotte Pike to a duplex near WSM's television station in West Nashville. Those particular duplexes had been military officer's quarters in the forties. I was twenty-four and still searching for that job that continually eluded me. But, Bennie and I were getting along well. He was always supportive and continued to assure me that I would find something and not to give up hope. Many days, hope was hard to find.

One Saturday afternoon, Bennie and I were watching TV while Michael played on the floor with his Tonka trucks. There was a knock at the door and I went to open it. There on the stoop was a jovial older man with a short beard. He said he would like to speak to us about buying some study Bibles. We sat down with him and I explained that we had a Bible and really didn't need another, but he pulled out several books anyway. One was on the history of religion while another was about the history of the Bible. The more I looked, the more intrigued I was. But we were strapped for money. We told the gentleman that I was looking for work and wished we could buy them, but felt we couldn't.

The elder man asked if he could pray with us. Of course we let him. As we bowed our heads, he prayed the sweetest prayer for God to bless us and help me find a job. My eyes were filled with tears as I touched his arm when we all said amen.

The man then suggested we buy the books, that God would provide a way. So, with what little money we had, we purchased those books and hugged the old man as he turned to leave. Just moments later, just after our door closed, Bennie looked out and could not find the old man.

"Where did he go?" Bennie asked.

I went to the window to look and I could not see him on the sidewalk, on the street, or anywhere else. We didn't see a car, or hear a car leave. It was if he had vanished into thin air. Bennie and I talked about the man often, and we always wondered who the stranger was and if he could have been an angel.

The next Monday morning when Bennie got to work, Mary Catherine told him that Monument still had an opening for receptionist. It seems they were having a hard time selecting a woman who could please all those important men. By now, Rick Blackburn was at Columbia Nashville and a new general manager, Paul Lovelace, was in the job. There were a lot of other changes at the executive level as well. John Dorris, who later went on to become a very successful artist manager, did my initial interview this time around. I guess I said the right things this time because I passed his interview process and was ushered across the hall. I wondered about the salesman's prayer a few days before, and how odd it was that the job became open.

My final interview was to be conducted by Lura Bainbridge, who was married to Fred Foster, owner of the label. Talk about beautiful and intimidating. Lura was a tall, slender beauty with long blond hair. She was wearing a beautiful suit, cleavage exposed, expensive jewelry, and four inch heels. I had never in my life met a woman like her; I had only seen women like that in the movies. She made me more nervous than any of the men I had interviewed with.

Apparently, the last few receptionists who were hired had not worked out so Lura was to make the final decision this time. She seemed to like me. She asked a few easy questions and then offered me the job. I guess six times is a charm—or at least it is persistency. After two years of looking, I finally had a job and the people seemed to be really nice. My salary, however, wasn't so great. After paying my car payment and for child care, I had ninety-six dollars left over. Not a lot of money for a month's work, but it was a paycheck.

It was at this point I came to another crossroad. A week into my new job at Monument, Channel 5 called to offer me a job as their receptionist. I was excited, and yet scared. Two job offers in two weeks. I must finally be getting something right. Since television was where I had dreamed of being, I inquired about the starting salary. It paid twenty-five dollars less per week than I was making at Monument. Since I only cleared ninety-six dollars a month at the label, I would have worked for nothing at the TV station. I politely declined the Channel 5 offer and stayed at Monument.

I really didn't want any more change in my life. I had just started Michael in daycare and it was difficult to leave him each morning. Often, he hung on the daycare's fence and cried, "Momma, don't leave me." I cried all the way to work. The teachers told me that he was fine once I was out of sight but I was never sure about that. I felt like I was abandoning him.

At work, as a receptionist, my only responsibility was to answer eight incoming lines and screen guests. I was bored to death. I asked for a typewriter. I volunteered to take on work from other departments. I offered to stay late to help, and earned overtime while learning more about the business. I was taught how to calculate session checks (those intricate payments to studio musicians) and royalty statements. I typed letters and contracts, and stayed after hours to assist John Dorris, the vice president of finance. In addition to the label that Fred owned, he also co-owned Combine Music Group with Bob Beckham.

Combine Music was one of the prominent music publishing companies of the day. Many artists who recorded for Monument Records were also signed as songwriters to Combine. Tony Joe White, Billy Swan, Kris Kristofferson, Wanda Jackson, Mickey Newberry, Dolly Parton, and Larry Gatlin were just a few of the artist songwriters there.

Another Combine songwriter, Dennis Linde, had songwriting credits that include "Burning Love" recorded by Elvis Presley, "Callin' Baton Rouge" (Garth Brooks), "Walkin' a Broken Heart (Don Williams), "Goodbye Earl" (Dixie Chicks), "Queen of My Double Wide" (Sammy Kershaw), "Bubba Shot the Jukebox" and "It Sure is Monday" (Mark Chesnutt). Linde's credentials started in the seventies and continue to this day as artists in all genres of music have recorded his songs.

Dennis married Bob Beckham's daughter, and Bob was an artist in his own right. Beckham was born in Stratford, Oklahoma and released two Top 40 singles of his own ("Just as Much as Ever" in 1959 and "Crazy Arms" in 1960) on Decca Records before joining Fred Foster in the launch of Combine Music Publishing. Beckham had a special ability to hear a hit song regardless of its genre. He and Fred Foster were Nashville visionaries who have yet to see the industry truly recognize their lasting contributions.

The Combine office was just two blocks from Monument Records, so writers and artists were always popping in to play a song or show up for a meeting with Fred. I watched. I listened. I asked questions about how things worked. My "college" was now my day-to-day job and I soaked up everything I could learn.

Many people who had been on the Row for a while said that the basement of the Combine building was haunted. Apparently, a lady who had owned the old house at the turn of the century was a big gardener. Many of the writer rooms were in the basement, and several of the writers told the same story of smelling the scent of flowers in the room and turning to see a woman in the hallway. When they got up to look for her, she was always gone. I think I would have found myself a new writer room had I seen the flower lady.

For the next three years, I got to know many of the artist writers who recorded there. Larry Gatlin (of the Gatlin Brothers and "All the Gold in California" fame) wrote for Combine Music and recorded for Monument Records. Larry often came in and sat on the steps to sing me a song he had just written and wanted Fred to hear. Sometimes, Larry showed up with his brothers Rudy and Steve to sing a song or visit with the staff. It was exciting to see our singles racing up the charts and hear them on local radio stations.

In 1975, Monument released Gatlin's first major hit with his composition, "Broken Lady." It reached #5 on the *Billboard* Hot Country Songs chart in 1976, around the time I went to work for the label. The song was so successful that Larry won a Grammy award for the song in 1977 for Best Country Song. A new album, *High Time*, was released in 1976. Brothers Steve and Rudy made their first appearance on Larry's 1976 album *Larry Gatlin with Family & Friends*. They were featured on some of Gatlin's other hits during the late 1970s, notably "I Don't Wanna Cry," "Love Is Just a Game," and "Statues Without Hearts," and by the late 70s Larry Gatlin & The Gatlin Brothers had become household names.

While at the label, I had the opportunity to meet many other stars as well. The first time I met legendary singer Roy Orbison, I could hardly believe my eyes. This quiet, soft-spoken man was so gentle and kind. Unlike some of the celebrities or executives who came in for meetings, Roy always treated me with respect. I will always remember and treasure that. Most of Roy's success at Monument was before I worked there, but he often visited Fred Foster as a friend, and for advice.

While I have thrown and attended many industry soirees in my career, my first industry party was a big one. Fred Foster held it in honor of Kris Kristofferson and Rita Coolidge. Kris and Rita had married in 1973 and released a highly successful album called *Full Moon*. The Monument party was a festive affair with champagne and candlelight, and the staff spent weeks getting the office ready for the event. I was assigned to stay downstairs and greet the guests as they arrived, then usher them upstairs to Fred's suite of offices where the party was being held. It was the most beautiful event I had ever seen, and the first of many in my future. The highlight for me was when I felt something cold hit my neck. I looked up to the balcony as Kristofferson apologized for tipping his drink and dropping a cube of ice on me. I wish I could have frozen that cube of ice in time, along with the memory.

There were several people at Monument who influenced my life and career. Paul Lovelace, who was the general manager, used to come out front to the lobby to talk to me. Paul's background had been in radio promotion. He always encouraged and counseled me with much needed advice. John Dorris, our financial comptroller, suggested I go into accounting and get my CPA license.

"You can make a six figure salary," he said. "Few jobs pay a woman that kind of money."

At the time, he was right. But while I had the aptitude for accounting, it was not something I dreamed about doing. I had tried my hand at singing jingles, took some acting classes, and had photos made for modeling. I dabbled in a lot of my interests but nothing was surfacing for me to build a career. I was seeking direction and not having any luck in figuring out what I truly wanted.

One night, Paul gave me some advice that changed my life and started me down the path to a career that would become more than I could ever envision. Listening to me struggle with indecision, he sat down in front of me for one of our late afternoon chats, and gave me some crystal clear advice.

"You are very, very talented," he said. "You can do many things well, but until you focus on just one area of expertise and become great at that one thing, you will never be successful. You also try too hard to please everyone around you and need to think more about what pleases you."

Then he added that he had something he wanted to share with me. He reached into his briefcase and pulled out a paperback book by Og Mandino, *The World's Greatest Salesman*. "It's pretty simple reading, and you are going to ask why in the world did Paul give this to me to read, but stick with it until the end and you will understand."

I later found that Paul had given the book to countless friends and business associates over the years. I took it home with me and read it all the way through that same evening. As Paul had warned, when I started reading the book I wondered why he had given it to me. But with each passing page I read the words and then it happened. The words took on a special meaning and I became very excited. I adopted the principles of the book and made them my own. The biggest change was that I began to look at others with love, including myself. I gave with no expectation of anything in return. That book changed my life. In the years ahead, I bought many copies of *The World's Greatest Salesman* to share with my own staff and friends. I am unsure of its effect on others, but I am confident of its effect on me.

I met a lot of new people at Monument, which was one of Bennie's goals for me in getting a job. One person was a "promotion man," Sheriff Tex Davis. Tex was exceptionally interesting to me because I had never met a person with this job before. Born William Douchette, he created the on-air name of Sheriff Tex Davis when he got his first radio job at country station WLOW in Norfolk, Virginia. He thought that name would work better than his real name in country radio. The name stuck. He was also a writer of the song "Be-Bop-a-Lula," recorded and made famous by Gene Vincent.

In 1967, Tex moved to Nashville to head the promotion department for Monument Records. Label promotion people are responsible for calling radio stations to encourage disc jockeys and radio programmers to add a song to their play list, and Tex was one of the best. Back in the seventies, and well into the late nineties, radio programmers had the autonomy to decide what music they played on their individual stations. Today, due to mergers, most stations no longer have that ability. Decisions about what listeners hear on a given radio station are often made on a corporate level.

Tex promoted the careers of Kris Kristofferson, Jeannie Sealy, and Dolly Parton, among others, and was probably in his late fifties by the time I met him. He was a burly fellow with a mustache who talked really loud. When he was on the phone making calls to country stations, I could hear him all the way out in the lobby. Some of the language was not appropriate for repeating, but I will tell you that Tex Davis was passionate about the songs he promoted. The tone he took with his programmers was not a style I adopted when I began to call on radio stations a few years later. And, while it wouldn't work for most promoters, it was the Sheriff's style.

One of Tex's best friends was Frank Leffell, who was then vice president of promotion for Mercury Records. Tex and Frank would go to lunch about twelve-thirty every day. They'd have a few drinks at lunch, return to the office around three-thirty, and Tex would depart for his home in Hendersonville shortly thereafter. No one other than me seemed to notice that his hours in the office were not as long as the rest of us. Maybe that was because he was always able to get those songs up the chart.

One day I was in the lobby answering the phones and greeting guests when a visitor arrived and asked to see Tex. I rang his office to inform him of his visitor's name and that he was requesting to see him. Tex yelled, "Tell him I'm not here." Wondering how I would professionally pass along this information to the gentleman without lying, I hung up the phone and turned to the visitor. Before I was able to speak, his guest replied, "I heard" and turned to leave. Despite his age and foreboding presence, Tex was good to me. He took time to talk to me and became a friend whom I loved very much. Tex died on August 29, 2007 after a long illness. He was ninety-three.

I found that the music business was, at times, a little like the old west. You never knew what was going to happen from one day to the next. Colorful characters were always stopping in for meetings with one of the executives. Monument's offices were beautiful and complete with a kitchen that the staff used. Tommy Jennings, Waylon's brother, recorded for Monument and used to come to the office all the time. He was quite the flirt, and made me more than a little nervous because he was one of those men who could quietly get into my space before I saw it happening.

One morning I was in the kitchen fixing a Diet Dr. Pepper and had the freezer door open to get some ice. The door hid my view of anyone who might walk into the kitchen. When I closed the door, there, inches away from my face, was Tommy Jennings. He grabbed my breasts with both hands and said, "I don't think you are wearing a bra." I was, of course, but that was beside the point. Jerking away from him, I vacated the kitchen and informed John Dorris that in the future, he needed to keep Tommy away from me as I had just been given a "physical exam" in the kitchen. John and Fred had some words with Tommy, and I ceased to see him in the office much after that. When he did come in, though, he was the perfect gentleman. I guess their little talk had some effect on him.

However, Tommy's kitchen visit made me vigilant in watching for him around every corner.

CHAPTER 6

Life or Death

About a year into the Monument job I began to suffer bouts of stomach pain that were almost incapacitating. After we had been in Nashville for a couple of years, Bennie and I had needed a family doctor. A friend of Bennie's, and a great radio announcer, Keith Bilbrey, recommended that I see his doctor. By this time I had actually been to Dr. Chikoniah several times. He was also the doctor I worked for three whole days before escaping the cattiness of his staff. So when I began to have bouts of pain in 1977, and at the urging of friends and label associates, I went to see Dr. Chickoniah for an evaluation. He diagnosed me with gall stones and recommended immediate surgery. He suggested I do it before I had another flair up that could prove to be life threatening.

Being a twenty-five-year-old woman, I was concerned about scars and expressed this to him. Dr. Chickoniah recommended a specific surgeon. He told me this man was a specialist who did a cosmetic incision that would leave very little scarring.

"Your scar will be smaller than a two inch scratch and will be barely visible," said Dr. Chickoniah.

Surgery, I learned, would require five to eight days in the hospital and a few weeks after that to recuperate. But my doctor made me feel that surgery was not only necessary, it was urgently needed.

By this time Michael was an active five-year-old and doing well in pre-school. I thought about Michael a lot with regard to the health concerns expressed by my doctor. We had some months earlier moved into a small house on Nashua Lane in West Nashville, and Michael had made friends with the neighborhood children. Our street was at the back of the sub-division, so traffic was light and many of the children rode bikes up and down the street in front of our house. The family next door had four boys and one of them was Michael's age. It was the perfect chance for him to play in the evening before dinner. At night, I tucked Michael into bed and read a story until his eyes were ready and the sandman stole him away. He was big into Star Wars, and his room was decorated with all of the characters from the movie.

Hours after I spoke with Dr. Chickoniah I tucked Michael into sleep, then sat down to discuss the surgery with Bennie. Together, we decided I should schedule the surgery now, and not wait until I had another flare up. A day or so later I met with the surgeon at his office and he explained the procedure. He assured me that I would not have a scar and there should be no complications.

I called my mom and she arranged for Sherlene to take care of Michael at Momma's house. Momma felt it would be easiest for her to drive back and forth to Nashville and have Michael there with Sherlene. She'd come down for the surgery, and then visit me in the hospital every day or two until I was able to go home. That way, Michael would be settled in one place and she wouldn't have to worry about his care. I wasn't fully comfortable with Sherlene caring for Michael, but it seemed the best option at the time.

Within days, I entered Nashville Memorial Hospital. When I arrived, early in the morning, I was prepped for the procedure and sedated. Then I heard nurses inquiring about the surgeon's whereabouts. They seemed concerned that he was not in the hospital. It seemed like hours passed. Finally a nurse said, "We found him." Only then was I wheeled into surgery and put under total sedation.

When I woke up after the surgery, I could not see. I could hear my mother saying my name, but I couldn't see her. Momma kept saying that I was deathly white, and I heard her ask the nurse if that was normal. The nurse then told her they almost lost me in the operating room. I thought I had only been under for a few minutes, but Momma said I had been gone almost six hours.

Many hours later I woke up again and my vision was back to normal. When the surgeon finally checked me, he said everything looked great. Momma and Bennie had gone home for the evening because I had told them I would be okay and did not need them to stay. But before daybreak, I began to experience searing pain under both shoulder blades. The pain got worse if I reclined. As a result, I could not lie down to sleep. Instead, I sat in a hospital chair by my bedside and slept a few minutes at a time. As the hours passed, the pain worsened. By the time Bennie came the next morning I was on the brink of tears. I felt the pain I was experiencing was not normal.

I expressed concern to my nurses and insisted that x-rays be made to determine the cause. Finally, one of the nurses came in to wheel me to x-ray. She said that everything appeared normal, but because I had so much pain, x-rays would be taken as a precautionary measure. After the x-rays were read, the surgeon came in to assure me that nothing was found and that I must have air trapped inside from the abdominal surgery.

"You will be fine in a few days," he said, "and I will see you at my office for a checkup in a week."

Eight miserable days after surgery, it was time to be discharged. I went to get dressed for the trip home and could not zip the jeans I had worn into the hospital. I assumed that my abdominal swelling would go down in a few days, but it did not. I continued to grow larger and larger until I was the size of an over-due pregnant woman. As my stomach extended further and further, so increased the pain.

My bilirubin count also increased, and the whites of my eyes turned yellow. I became horribly jaundiced. Bilirubin is a brownish yellow substance found in bile. It is produced when the liver breaks down old red blood cells and is passed through the body via the intestines. When bilirubin levels are high, the skin and the whites of the eyes appear yellow. In addition to the excruciating pain, this was the first sign of something terribly wrong.

"No worries," I was told by surgeon. "This should all clear up in a few days."

In my weekly doctor visits, my surgeon said it was rare to have a surgical complication like mine. "But," he said. "You will be all right in a few weeks. Sometimes air gets trapped inside, or a patient retains fluids." He prescribed a diuretic for water retention and told me to come back in a week. He said he was going on vacation but I would be fine. He would see me when he returned.

But I wasn't all right. I was dying, and didn't know it. I believe the surgeon knew, but had no intention of telling me. The pain medication that was prescribed to me and taken every six hours lasted only sixty to ninety minutes. I couldn't sleep. I couldn't eat. Drinking water caused me to suffocate and I gasped for air. My stomach was growing larger by the day, even though I could not eat or drink anything. I could not breathe well, and when I did I could hear a scary rattle in my chest. I constantly wheezed and gasped for breath as my lungs filled with fluid.

I also became so thin that it hurt my hips to sit. My knees and elbows became bony and ached when I moved. I could barely stand long enough to use the bathroom, or get out of the bathtub, and could feel my strength ebbing away. Sometimes in the dark hours of the night when the world was asleep, I felt abandoned and alone, and when I looked for hope, I found none. I prayed to die. I prayed to get well, and I prayed to understand what was happening.

My insides from my groin to my neck felt as if someone had placed burning coals of fire inside and was stirring them with a hot poker. It was difficult to walk because the slightest movement sent excruciating pain through my entire body. Week after week passed and I was not improving. Each week I made my trek to the surgeon, where he jostled my stomach and heard the liquid slosh inside. He only prescribed more diuretics.

Most people don't understand suicide. They believe it to be a sin and condemn the person who cheats life and all those who love them as a coward. I now understand there are circumstances where we reach a decision because we can find no answers outside the need to be free of the agony that burns within us. Cancer patients in their final days understand this. Nearing the end of those weeks, I understood what brings a person to that threshold. Thankfully, I reached the other side of my agony and am still walking in this life. Some do not make it. I don't agree or condone suicide. There are always answers. There is always hope. But hope is sometimes hard to find when every ounce of your being in blinded by searing pain twenty-four hours a day, seven days a week.

I am a strong woman, but even strong women break. Several times during that six weeks following surgery, the agony became so bad that I decided to end my life. Three times I went to our bathroom cabinet to see if I had enough medication to commit suicide. Three times I looked in the mirror and saw a woman who could not leave behind her five-year-old son. I had to live for him. I had promised him I would be okay.

My decision not to commit suicide wasn't for me. I didn't care about dying. That would actually be a relief. I knew my life after death would be a better life than here on earth. What I cared about was my little boy. If I took my life, Michael would grow up thinking I was a coward. He would always think I didn't love him enough to stay in this world, and that simply was not true. I loved my son far more than the searing agony I had lived with for six weeks. I wasn't a coward. I had faced down too many guns and knives and too many harsh words to walk away from him by ending my life. So I lived one minute at a time, one prayer at a time.

During this time in my life I used to go home to Kentucky almost every weekend. I had not been home in six weeks so I asked Bennie to drive me to see Momma. My brother, Shelby, and sister, Sherlene, came to Momma's house to see me, but all I could do was lie on the couch in agony. By now, I looked like a ten-month pregnant woman and only had one wrap around dress that I could wear. None of my other clothes fit.

Momma cried when she saw me and asked what she could do to help. I didn't know if there was anything she could do. Momma took bath towels, held them in hot water, and draped them across my stomach in an attempt to relieve my agony. My brother and sister sat with me with tears in their eyes and fear on their faces. I turned to my brother and begged Shelby to pray for me. I had begun to turn a light shade of gray and my eyes were yellow and sunk into my head.

Tears pooled in his eyes and he said, "If God isn't hearing your prayers, why do you think he would hear mine?"

I needed God to hear Shelby's prayers. I needed Him to help me, and I needed all the faith I could muster from those who loved me more than life itself.

Shelby suggested I speak to another doctor and called his childhood friend's dad, who was a doctor in Scottsville. Shelby had gone to school with Dr. Halcomb's son, Joseph. Shelby had played in a band with Joe and was often at his home during high school.

When he had Dr. Halcomb on the line, Shelby told him about the problems I was having and asked if he would speak to me. He agreed and Shelby handed me the phone. I told him about the surgery, my symptoms, the excruciating pain, the fluid, the jaundice, and swelling. I told him that my surgeon said it was normal, and that sometimes there are complications like mine.

For a moment, there was silence. Then Dr. Halcomb told me that he could not diagnose me over the phone, nor could he tell me what was wrong. He did tell me to get to a doctor immediately, because what I was experiencing was not a normal complication of surgery. Hearing those words gave me the strength to seek help outside the doctors who had been treating me. I had lost so much weight (except for my protruding stomach) that I had to carry pillows to sit on and rest against.

Hanging up the phone, I told my family about the conversation. While they seemed relieved that I had spoken to someone who was wiser than we were, there was also a fear that it might be too late to save me. A few hours later, Bennie and I gathered my pillows and headed to the car to return to Nashville. I remember looking at all of them that Sunday evening, wondering if that would be the last time I saw my family.

We got home about ninety minutes later and I put Michael to bed while Bennie went to our bedroom to get some sleep. I waddled back to the living room couch where I could prop myself upright. I was still unable to lie down flat because of the pain, and from the internal fluid and weight that suffocated me when I reclined.

That night as I sat in our lonely living room I had a strange feeling that I was coming to the end of my life. The night wore on into the early hours of morning, and I began to pray. Over and over again, I recited the 23rd Psalm while I tried to take my mind off the searing pain, and I recalled what Momma taught me about prayer.

"You have to be willing to accept whatever God has planned for you," Momma said. "You can't pray for what you want, but rather what God wants for you. You have to believe. You have to accept *His* will."

I knew I was at the end of all hope, so I prayed. But I stopped praying the same prayer I had been praying for six weeks. I stopped praying to die. I stopped praying to live. Instead, I started to pray a different prayer. I asked God to look at me and into my heart. I asked him to listen to my prayer and do what He chose to do with me. I prayed, "If it's your will that I live, let me live. If it's your will that I die, let me die. If a man caused me to be this sick and only a man can cure me, then help me find a doctor who can make me well." I also prayed, "If I have anything I am supposed to do that I have not accomplished, let me live and guide my steps to where I need to be."

The living room in our little house was always bright from a streetlight outside our window. But on this night, light shadows began to fill the room. Just as so many years before, when my mother prayed for our family to be spared, I felt a peace begin to flow through my body. I wanted to rejoice, but didn't know why. I could still feel the constant searing pain, but suddenly it was bearable.

It was then that I saw a presence in the room, there in the corner of the living room next to the window. Was it an angel that God sent to bring me a message? Or, was it Christ in a vision to warm my soul and give me the strength to live? Was it a message that my prayer had been heard and answered? Did He look as I imagined Christ to look only because I trusted and believed He would come to me in my darkest hours?

Warmth spread through my body and overwhelmed my senses. It was as if a blanket had been wrapped around me and I was being held tightly in someone's strong arms. In that quiet moment before dawn, I knew something had changed. In that moment, I knew it was not my time to die. I knew I would live. It was August 16, 1977 and I was now confident that a long life lay before me. To this day, I have no doubt of what I saw in the wee hours of the morning, or that my prayer was answered. As quickly as He appeared, the shadowy figure began to fade. And as He left, my pain began to subside. I awaited the sunrise and what the new day would bring.

The next morning, I felt compelled to ask Bennie to drive me to the Monument building so I could see my friends at the office. I had not seen any of them since I left the hospital some six weeks before. As I walked into the accounting area and the girls saw my face, their expressions changed. While they appeared to be glad to see me, there was shock on their faces, too. Like my family's reaction, they saw changes in me that I could not even recognize. I clumsily sat down, adjusting my pillows and knobby knees, and

Linda Scott, one of our accounting personnel jumped up from her desk and left the room. She returned with Fred Foster in tow.

What I did not know was that Fred had been instrumental in saving the life of Tex Davis's wife, Betty, some years before when she was seriously ill. Fred took one look at me and said, "This girl is dying. I have seen death before. I see it in her eyes."

As Fred stood in the doorway, tears welled up in his eyes. He told me to sit still, that he was going to find help for me. Fred first called the chaplain at Vanderbilt University and asked him who the best internist in Nashville was. Fred told the chaplain that he had a woman in his office that was dying. He needed the best doctor in Nashville and he needed him or her immediately—no excuses.

Fred was told to call an internist by the name of Dr. Robert Johnson. Fred made the call and secured an appointment for me. I also spoke by phone to Dr. Bob. He asked several questions before passing me along to his personal nurse to gather additional data for his files. The nurse asked me to come by the office immediately and let them pull blood work. Then I was to meet Dr. Johnson at West Side Hospital at six P.M. that evening when he made rounds.

Little did I know at the time, but were it not for Fred Foster stepping in and making that call, I would most certainly have died. Miracles are delivered in all kinds of packages. Sometimes they are handed to us by people we know and love. Sometimes God handles miracles through the talents of a doctor's hands. One phone call and one man's connections changed the course of my future more than I could realize at the time.

Shirley Scott, one of the women who worked in the accounting department, drove me to the Dr. Johnson's office. Bennie had to cut some radio commericals that afternoon and was unable to take me. After my blood was pulled, Shirley drove me back to our little house on Nashua Lane. She looked at me sadly as she backed out of the driveway and headed back to work. I could see the fear in her face as she, too, realized she might never see me again.

It was several hours until I was scheduled to meet Dr. Johnson. I waited, and waited. I was resting on the couch when a newscaster broke in with a bulletin that Elvis Presley had been found dead. It was August 17, 1977. As stunned as I was by the news of his sudden death, the only thought that crossed my mind was "everyone has their time to die." I was glad my time was not today, although it easily could have been.

When Bennie returned home that afternoon, he suggested I get ready so we could head to the hospital. I didn't want to go. I had gone downhill that afternoon and was too weak. I hurt too much to move and was having difficulty breathing. At his insistence, I pulled on my blue wrap around dress, found my pillows, grabbed Michael's little five-year-old hand, and slowly walked the short distance from our front door to the car.

As directed by Dr. Johnson's staff, we parked near the emergency entrance of the hospital. When we entered, nurses took one look at me and began to scramble. I must have looked like a walking dead woman. One nurse took hold of my arm, and said, "You're burning up with fever. How high is your temperature?" I didn't even know I had a temperature. I had no idea of anything except for the searing pain I felt every second of the day and night. They rushed me first to x-ray. Technicians drew more blood. Nurses hooked me to IVs and began to push liquids into my frail arms.

Before long Dr. Johnson came in and sat beside me. He reviewed the charts and the numbers and asked me the same questions twenty times over. He told me he would be right back and stepped outside to find Bennie. Doing so, he asked Bennie if we were Catholic. Trembling, Bennie replied, "No. We are not. Why are you asking? Is it that bad?" Dr. Johnson told him to get his pastor and any family that might want to see me. "She may not make it through the night."

Dr. Johnson had reviewed the blood tests and later told me that he could not believe I was able to walk at all. He said when he spoke to me by phone that I had never let on how very sick I was, and he could not believe I had survived as long as I had.

"You are a strong woman to have withstood this pain," he said. "Without seeing you and looking at your test results, I would never have known it from your voice."

One of the nurses said the doctor was attending a black tie affair that evening and would be making quick rounds before leaving. But Dr. Johnson never left that night. He stayed by my side checking vitals and talking to me about what to expect. His tuxedo hung somewhere downstairs for a party he would never attend.

After a few hours, his voice became quiet and he informed me that I needed surgery again. He sat on my bed, drew pictures and explained everything in great detail. I had no Vitamin K, no clotting factor, no potassium. The diuretic I had taken had depleted me of those nutrients. All the necessary ingredients for life were gone from my body. What nutrients I did have were in my IV along with antibiotics. But surgery was a must—and soon. He asked if I trusted him and I said that I did.

"I will only recommend one surgeon to operate on you," Dr. Johnson said. "He is the best thoracic surgeon in Nashville and is the only surgeon I would let cut on me."

"It's in your hands," I said.

"No," he replied, "It's in God's hands, too."

The next morning at daybreak I met Dr. Robert Sadler. Like Dr. Johnson, he sat at my side when he described what he intended to do surgically. He said he had no idea what he would find but there was no other choice but to do exploratory surgery. He patted my hand and with tears in his eyes told me he'd do his best to take care of me. I was prepped and rolled into surgery that same morning. Some ten hours after surgery began, I woke up in intensive care with tubes in my nose and throat and IVs in every arm. My arms were black and blue from my elbows to my wrists.

Suddenly, I saw Dr. Sadler approach my intensive care bed. He spoke to me for a few minutes as he looked into my eyes and checked my blood pressure. After seeing that I was awake enough to hear what he had to say, he explained what he had found. According to Dr. Sadler, the first surgeon had left three large c-clamps on my common bile duct, and those had caused my duct to rupture and leak bile into my abdominal cavity. I had developed an infection called bile peritonitis.

Acute peritonitis, I learned, can be produced by inflammation of abdominal organs, irritating substances from a perforated gallbladder or gastric ulcer, rupture of a cyst, or irritation from blood, as in cases of internal bleeding. Immediate and intense pain is felt at the site of infection, followed usually by fever, vomiting, and extreme weakness. The abdomen becomes rigid and sensitive to the touch. The patient may suffer mental confusion, fever, prostration, or shock. Although antibiotics can reduce the mortality rate of acute peritonitis, the infection should be treated and controlled immediately. It can be fatal if neglected.

Dr. Johnson said death usually occurs within thirty-six hours of its development. I had lived six weeks. Because of the intense infection, all they could do was drain one and a half gallons of poison from my system, rinse me with saline and close me up. Then, he told me that I needed one more operation. It was only then that I began to cry. I needed another surgery to remove the clamps, but they could not perform it yet because I would die if one drop of the poison that filled me got into my blood stream.

"Get some rest," he said. "I'll check on you later."

One by one, my family came into the room holding back tears. After Bennie, Momma was the first. Then surprisingly, I saw my daddy's face. I had no idea he was there. Momma had found him and brought him to Nashville. She had apparently told Daddy that if he wanted to see his daughter again, he had one chance and he better get in the car with her right then, because she was headed to Nashville.

I cried because of the tubes, and because I saw so much love and fear in their eyes. The doctors and nurses explained that it might be three weeks before I would be well enough to withstand another operation. They planned to give me vitamins and antibiotics to strengthen my immune system, and even then there was no guarantee.

But, it wasn't three weeks. It was seven days later that Dr. Sadler operated again to undo and repair the damage within me. The doctors and nurses couldn't understand how I healed so rapidly. I was a miracle. Never had they witnessed such a recovery. It wasn't supposed to be possible. I spent more than a month in West Side Hospital, three of those weeks in intensive care, struggling to live. When the nurses thought I was sleeping, I often heard them talking about how horrible it was that any doctor could do this to someone. They talked about his carelessness and how he needed to be in prison, and couldn't believe that I lived through the trauma.

Momma came to see me almost every day and said they were talking about me on the Scottsville radio station, asking people to pray. Pray they did. I can't begin to explain it to anyone who hasn't stood on the threshold of death, but I could hear people praying for me. When I closed my eyes it sounded like a million angelic voices lifting me up in prayer.

During those three weeks, I had a number of visitors. Larry Gatlin and Larry Jon Wilson were two Monument recording artists who stopped by. Other friends from work also stopped in to pay their regards.

One night after I was finally moved from intensive care to a private room, I lay in my hospital bed reading my Bible. Dr. Johnson popped in for his usual doctor's round and saw me reading.

"Are you finding any answers in there?" he asked.

I told him that I was finding lots of answers and that he was one of them. That's when he sat down in a chair and began to wipe his eyes.

"It's not me, but God who saved you," he said. "Until I met you, I had never witnessed a miracle in my entire medical career. But with you, I did. Every day I watch people die and I can't save them. One of my patients died today from cancer, and I could do nothing for her. I feel so inadequate. Thank you for what you said, but I am not the reason you are alive."

"But you are," I said. "You are part of the miracle. Never doubt that. Sometimes God has to use people to perform His miracles. A doctor did the damage and a doctor had to undo what was done. God just kept me alive long enough to find the right doctor."

Dr. Johnson gave my hand an extra squeeze before he left.

During that time when I could reach out and touch the hand of Death, I reached inside myself and found new strength. When I found myself facing that foreboding darkness before the dawn my faith in God only grew stronger. I had heard the prayers of loved ones, had felt the prayers of strangers. I had witnessed a miracle in my own life, and I changed as I realized how fragile life truly is.

Through my ordeal I learned that life is like a kite, suspended by a spider's web waving in the breeze. It could snap at any moment. But my life didn't snap. I was alive. There was a second chance for me and I knew God had something planned. In the meantime, I reached the other side stronger than before, and a far better person. When I left that hospital I had more compassion and understanding. I was less frustrated with petty jealousies and the many small things that had tripped me up before. I also began to appreciate each and every day as I saw the world through fresh eyes.

By this time I had been absent from work for three months. Monument continued to pay me, even though I had only been there a year when I had the initial surgery. The people at Monument were more than just co-workers. They were family. Fred and John had told me not to worry about the job, but to focus on getting well. When I finally returned to work in October of 1977, I was promoted to administrative assistant to John Dorris. I worked on budgets and artist contracts, set appointments, and learned everything that John could teach me. The next few years were troubling times for the label, as it struggled to keep itself solvent. To add to the mix, Fred and Lura Bainbridge divorced. Fred began to date a young singer and they later married. Soon there were a lot of closed-door meetings and calls from the banks. I knew something was wrong and prodded John to give us answers.

In January 1979, John explained the problem to the staff. He said the label had to cut back. Even though I had anticipated it and thought I would be prepared for it, I was not. I was one of seven people who were released that day, and I was devastated. These people had stood by my side through my illness, and were the only family and friends I had in Nashville. What was I to do? I was at another crossroad, but this time I couldn't read the signs.

• • •

With encouragement from friends and my doctors, Bennie and I sued the surgeon who had left the clamps inside of me. When my lawyers pulled the hospital records, it was discovered that the x-rays I had insisted on having done did indeed show the metal clamps. The surgeon knew they were there *and said nothing*. No insistence of a second surgery to correct the error. He waited for my life to slip away, perhaps hoping my family would believe my death to be a rare complication from surgery. With my internists and thoracic surgeon prepared to testify, the claim was settled out of court. After the attorneys got their share, I had thirty-three thousand dollars left over. Bennie and I used part of it to buy a three-bedroom ranch house in a quiet West Nashville neighborhood a few months before Michael started first grade. Due to the complications of that surgery and the damage to my fallopian tubes, I was never able to have more children. I had always dreamed of a little girl, but that dream would not be fulfilled in my lifetime.

The Monument Records building on Music Row when I worked there. Today, it has been remodeled and houses Warner Chappell Music.

Fred Foster, Jimmy Bowen, and Ray Stevens (all of whom I worked with)

CHAPTER 7

RCA Records

I was twenty-seven years old and Bennie and I had been in Nashville five years. Hard to believe so much time had passed. Bennie had just changed jobs and was now working cross-town at WSIX-FM. Future National Association of Broadcasters Radio Hall of Fame personality Gerry House hosted the morning show and was also the program director for the station, so he was in charge of all the air personalities and staff. Michael was in first grade and when we could keep him in his seat, he seemed to excel. I often got calls from teachers who informed me that Michael sometimes got up, and walked out of the classroom and onto the playground without permission. He was smart, but his short attention span caused problems.

Bennie and I continued to have our differences. He was always supportive, but more and more he relied on me to be the strong one. He began to ask me to drive whenever we went out, and whenever we agreed to go to church on Sunday he always conveniently had a stomachache that morning. In later years, he informed me that he suffered from agoraphobia, which caused him tremendous difficulty. Agoraphobia is an anxiety disorder where a person has intense attacks of fear and anxiety outside places that are considered "safe," such as the home. At the time, however, neither Bennie nor I realized that he was struggling with this disorder.

Outside of his anxiety, Bennie loved radio, videography, and photography, and was an incredible talent at voice-over work who was beginning to do a lot of regional commercials. Bennie really was thriving in the major market radio world. When I came home with the news of Monument's down-sizing, Bennie assured me that I would find something else. He was right. The very week I was dismissed became a week that I indeed found something else.

Tom Rodden was a man I met when he worked at Monument with me. Tom was in charge of marketing and advertising, and interacted with our distribution and sales personnel. A few months after I started, Tom left to join *Record World* magazine as its editor-in-chief. Paul Lovelace and Tom were best friends, and when Paul had lunch with Tom the week of Monument's downsizing, Paul told Tom about my job loss. Paul was watching out for me and wanted to help me find a new position.

Networking is extremely important in any business. Were it not for Paul's connection and friendship with Tom, I might not have heard about the job opening at RCA Records. Tom then called to tell me he knew of a job in their promotion and marketing department. He had already placed a call to them and made them aware of me. They were expecting my call.

I followed up and called John Olsen in personnel and secured an interview on a snowy Friday afternoon in January 1979. John visited with me downstairs, and explained a little about the position. He then walked with me to the elevator where we headed up to the second floor to meet with Joe Galante, who was vice president of promotion and marketing.

Joe was responsible for the staff of people who called on radio and promoted all the records released on RCA. It was his job to strategize the release plan on each single, assuring that it reached its maximum position on the country *Billboard* charts. In addition, he developed marketing strategies for each of the album releases, and set goals for the publicity, promotion, and sales departments that created placement in retail outlets such as Best Buy and Target. He was a tough taskmaster, but he delivered results and in the major label record world, that is all that mattered.

Joe mentioned that the job entailed servicing product to radio stations (sending them music), researching and adding new stations to send music to, processing promotional record order forms, maintaining inventory levels in the record storage area, take tracking from the regionals, process and run tracking sheets, and relay information to and from Joe. Basically, when a country station called to ask for the new Waylon Jennings single, for example, it was my job to pull the single from the store room, then package and mail it. I also needed to maintain an inventory of all the singles, and reorder before we ran out.

When radio stations wanted albums to give away on the air, I was to investigate the station, make sure they were in a market large enough for us to approve the product, and then write up a promotional order. Since this was often ten to fifteen albums at a time, the manufacturing plant shipped them directly to the station.

The *Billboard* charts were based on the number of spins reported on each song in a given week. Our regional representatives then called me to let me know a specific station played the Waylon single twenty-five times that week. I'd look at my last week's tracking, and see the same station played the single twenty times the week before. That increase of five spins helped move the single up the chart. At that time, there were over two hundred fifty radio stations that reported to *Billboard* each week. It sounded like a tough job, but it was one I was ready for.

I asked what my title would be. Joe and John Olson, then head of personnel, looked at each other and said it was marketing secretary. They also told me it could be changed if that title bothered me. It did concern me, because with this job, I didn't feel like I was a secretary to anyone. They told me the title would be Coordinator of Marketing & Promotion, and I was fine with that. I was hired on the spot and told to report that next Monday. The best news was that I was making twenty-five dollars more per week than the job I had left at Monument two weeks before. I was now making a whopping one hundred seventy-five dollars each week.

Six months later, in the summer of 1979, the oil crisis struck. In those days records were made of vinyl, which was a by-product of the tar residue created by oil. Most people in the music business then recall Black Friday and the huge nationwide label cutbacks. While Nashville, Los Angeles, and New York were the centers of the music industry, there were many music sales reps and radio promoters who worked for a label, but lived in other parts of the country. These cuts affected thousands of people nationwide, as labels were asked to cut their staffs by at least ten percent.

All of a sudden, there were a lot of closed door meetings. Only six months into my job I began to fear that something was wrong. It reminded me of the tension I had seen at Monument the prior year. Then one afternoon, Joe finally gave me some news. He was moving me to the sales department to work for Dave Wheeler. He mentioned that I would also continue to handle my promotion and marketing responsibilities. The woman who I was replacing in the sales department was on vacation and would not know what was happening until her return.

Dave Wheeler was one of the sweetest, kindest people at RCA. He was probably in his fifties then and was very knowledgeable about the business. Best of all, Joe appeared to respect Dave immensely. Dave had worked his way up through the ranks and had experience both as a salesman and as a branch manager. His job at RCA was to deal with each of our branch managers, who in turn dealt with the sales force that placed our product into retail stores. Each week, Dave's department relayed the week's airplay, press clippings, and updates on each of the Nashville record releases.

I was thankful that both Dave and I had survived the cutbacks, but it was very hard for me to take on someone else's job before that person was told she was fired. When Dave's assistant returned from vacation on Monday morning, she was called in and let go. Downsized. Whatever you want to call it, she was gone. Even though I had less tenure, I stayed on, but was now handling both her job and mine. Two jobs; one salary. So, I picked up the sales secretary duties answering phones, talking with branch offices, learning to operate computers, and designing reports to incorporate all the data our office collected.

While I was terribly busy with my sales, promotion, and marketing responsibilities, it wasn't challenging. I dreamed of a job where I could have a title and an office instead of an open area outside the second floor elevator door. It was also hard for me to believe that the scared little girl who spent years looking for a job in Nashville was now working for one of the largest music corporations in America. I had only been working for three and a half years at this point, but my confidence and skills had grown immensely.

After six months of working with the regional promotion staff, I determined that was the best department for me. I believed I could call on radio stations and promote our music. So, I requested a meeting with Joe Galante, and asked him if I could do radio promotion.

"No woman has ever been successful calling on country radio stations," Joe said. But, he agreed to think about it over the weekend and give me an answer on Monday. He was a man of his word. On Monday, he informed me that I had his permission. All I needed to do was check with each of the regional reps to make sure they didn't have a problem with me calling on the reporters for *Radio & Records* Magazine and for *Gavin* Magazine reporters in their territories. If they didn't have an issue with it, he didn't either.

"If any woman can do this," said Joe, "I believe you can." Hearing Joe speak those words made me feel like I could do anything. I had the utmost respect for his vision and leadership, and for him to say that was huge for me.

So, I picked up a new job along with the job I started with and the job I inherited. In essence, I was now doing three jobs. No additional money, but I was sure making headway on additional responsibilities. I still did not have an office, but my spot right outside the elevator door did provide me one of the better vantage points for the comings and goings on that floor.

In my newest job, I completed a weekly radio tracking sheet that summarized all the airplay for the week. I also wrote a weekly report that summarized the weeks' activities and comments from staff and radio stations. At that time, RCA's promotion department was not structured the way it is today. There was not a vice president, national director, field director, and *then* regional reps. Joe Galante was the acting vice president of promotion and marketing, but he had his hands full running the day-to-day operation of the label. That meant there wasn't anyone who could train me to do promotion, no one I could be an apprentice to. I was just given the opportunity to do promotion along with all of my other responsibilities. I did not want to go to Joe and ask him how to do it because I had assured Joe I could handle it. I didn't want to ask the regionals how to do it, because I would be laughed out of the building.

So, I began to plan my strategy. I understood the needs of radio because Bennie had been in radio since he was fifteen. I also understood people. I was organized, and I figured I would talk to people the way I wanted to be talked to. I would be honest and passionate about the music I promoted. And you know what? I made it work.

Every day I called radio stations and asked for the music director, as this was the person who most often made the play list decisions for the station. Once I had them on the phone, I introduced myself and let them know I would be calling them each and every week. Early on, I asked questions about the station, their job, how long they had been there, etcetera. In subsequent weeks, I pulled more and more information, until I truly felt like I knew the person.

In each call, after some initial chit chat, I started to ask about our singles and how they were performing. Were they getting phone requests for the song? What did they think of the song? Was it something they felt they could play? Sometimes it was not a song the station felt they wanted to play and my job was to explore that further and find out what information they needed to get them to change their mind. I have often felt that radio promotion is like a lawyer pleading a case in court. The station rep says one thing, the label rep counters with information that agrees or contradicts, and the dance goes on until the music ends.

At times, the regional reps (regionals) were hard on me. We had one Texas regional, Wayne Edwards (who later managed Tracy Lawrence), who tried to get me fired at least twice a week, usually after he returned from too many drinks at lunch. He thought women were good for only one thing—and promotion wasn't it. In his mind, promotion was a man's job, and there were many arguments with him about what my place was and wasn't. In the music business, and most likely any business at that time, pretty women were easy targets for slanderous remarks. In years since, personnel departments have cautioned executives about what they can and cannot say, but those conversations didn't come along until the nineties, and after several major lawsuits had played out. Personally, I got a lot of sexual overtures and condescending comments from staff and radio personnel, and I was tricked into hotel rooms and slammed across a bed a few times, but I always escaped.

I saw the careers of several women sink after they filed sexual harassment claims. Every person has to follow their own instincts as to what is right for them. But from what I saw in the business, the woman never won—even if she won the case. Other labels would not hire her because they were afraid she would sue them, too. I heard the hallway chatter, and even saw a girl fired from RCA because she blew the whistle. It wasn't right, but I learned to keep my mouth shut.

I never allowed anyone to run over me or take advantage of me sexually, but I felt it best to keep my comments to myself. I tried not to let anything that was said or done interfere with my performance. As long as they didn't touch, I wouldn't sue or tell. That was the way I chose to handle harassment. As I grew in power, however, that advice changed. I did not want an employee of mine to suffer indignation or embarrassment at the hands of a peer or a superior in the workplace. But that is now and not back in the seventies.

I never told anyone about those harassing moments. Instead, I kept quiet and attempted to do a good job despite the jabs and the overtures. I wanted more than anything to excel at radio promotion and make a name for myself. The *R&R* and *Gavin* stations I called were all in smaller metro markets. Each US city (or market) is ranked according to population and purchasing power. New York, Los Angeles, and Chicago, for example, are ranked higher than Des Moines, Chattanooga, and Santa Fe. I called stations in market sizes 100 to 200. These were considered secondary stations. Most major stations reported to *Billboard*.

I made a lot of relationships with secondary radio personnel who later went on to hold jobs at major reporting stations. This was huge for me. By the time they became a *Billboard* reporter, I already knew and had been friends with them when no one else was calling on them. It gave me a big edge over my competition.

In addition, a lot of promotion people are known for stretching the truth. They will tell radio *anything* to get them to play the song. A label promoter might say a song was getting phone requests when it wasn't, or that it was selling huge numbers when boxes of records were coming back in returns. I decided early on that I would not be that type of promotion person.

Once, Joe asked me to call on a *Billboard* reporter in Pittsburgh. We had a horrible record by a brand new artist and he wanted me to call this station to see if I could get them to play it. After a little back and forth, the music director asked me if I liked the song. For a moment, there was dead silence. Then, I said, "No, I actually don't. But I hear lots of songs on the radio that I don't like. It's my job to convince you to give it a chance. If you play it enough to be heard and don't get anything on it, then you can drop it."

The man laughed and said he had never had a promotion person admit to him that they didn't like one of their own records. He said because of that, he would add it and let me know. He only played the song for about three weeks, but he gave both the song and me a chance. The icing on the cake was that he became a life long friend. My honesty ended up becoming my trademark, and took me to the pinnacle of success within the industry. But that would be a few years after my departure from RCA.

In the meantime, I worked three jobs for one salary and received a seven to ten percent raise every year. I never received that manager's title, even though I was doing the work of a manager and the secretarial work of two people. About three years after I started at RCA, I finally got a title change to Coordinator, Country Promotion and Sales. I was regularly praised for my work, and the words made me feel confident about my performance. The next day, for no apparent reason, the words of praise would change to something else. I was reminded that I "was nothing but a secretary and should not push for inclusion in everything the company did." While the notes and attitude hurt at the time, they also taught me what not to do should I ever attain an executive position.

In the fall of 1979, I gave a tape of a band I had heard on the radio to Joe Galante. I loved the lead singer's voice and thought they had potential. Joe was busy and wanted to pass the A&R (short for Artist and Repertoire) baton to Tony Brown, who was head of that department. The A&R department was responsible for finding new talent to sign to the label, So, Joe sent the tape back to me with a note that read: LET TONY LISTEN TO IT. Tony had grown up in southern gospel music and had played piano for Elvis Presley. He had also headed a pop imprint called Free Flight Records before Joe moved him to Nashville to head up our A&R department.

So, I sent the tape to Tony who sent it back with a note that read: I DON'T WANT TO SIGN A BAND. BANDS ALWAYS BREAK UP AND GIVE YOU MORE TROUBLE THAN THEY ARE WORTH. PASS. A few weeks later I learned that the band had been picked up by an independent label called MDJ Records and had released a song called "My Home's in Alabama." They had shortened their name from The Alabama Band to Alabama.

I rushed into Dave Wheeler's office late one day, all stirred up and waving the new *R&R*. At that time, they printed a page inside the weekly magazine with all of the reporting stations along with the songs they had added that week. I had highlighted all of the Alabama adds. We were struggling to get adds with artists we had on the RCA roster and this band was making it look easy.

Joe stepped into the room behind me and asked what I was talking about. I told him the band Tony had passed on had a tremendous amount of *R&R* adds, and showed him the sheet. I couldn't believe RCA had passed. I later learned that every label in town had passed. Joe asked if I still had the package. It was in my desk so I hurriedly pulled it out and handed it to Joe to take home that night. The next morning he asked if I could get in touch with the band. I said I would try.

First, I called Bennie. Bennie had interviewed Alabama's lead singer, Randy Owen, on his WSIX Radio show and still had his home number in Ft. Payne, Alabama. I called and spoke to Randy's wife Kelly. She was delightful and said that Randy and the boys were in Myrtle Beach rehearsing for a show. She suggested I call them at the Holiday Inn there and gave me the number.

When I called the hotel and asked for Randy Owen, the front desk attendant transferred my call. The phone rang a couple of times before a voice answered, "Sherwood Forest, Robin Hood speaking." I paused, and then asked for Randy Owen. There was a pause on the other end of the line before the man said, "This is Randy."

I then began to explain who I was and why I was calling, only to be met with dead silence. I told Randy that Joe Galante at RCA wanted to speak to him about signing the group, and again, there was dead silence. I wasn't sure what was wrong but I was not getting any feedback. Only when I told him I was married to Bennie Shipley who had done an interview with Randy a few weeks before did Randy become warmer to me. Randy then told me they had signed with a small independent label called MDJ Records. I got the name and number of the owner (and their then manager), Larry McBride, and told Randy that I would ask Joe to call Larry to discuss options.

The rest, as they say, is history. A few months later, the group signed with RCA. I became friends with all of the band members, but was especially close to Randy and Kelly Owen. When we finally met and got to know each other, Randy told me that after he hung up the phone that day at The Holiday Inn, all of the guys started jumping up and down on the beds with excitement. Bennie, Michael, and I made several trips to Fort Payne to stay with Kelly and Randy both in their first home, and then the larger home they built across the road. Despite their massive success, their personalities always remained the same. That is so rare in the entertainment business.

Alabama was beginning to have some major success when Bennie and I first spent the weekend with them at their house in Ft. Payne. It was a small house. Randy and Kelly had cut carpet remnants into squares and covered the walls to help keep out the cold weather. They used a wood-burning stove for heat and Kelly regularly cut wood while we were there.

One morning she had on a flannel shirt and rollers in her hair as we were all stacking some of the wood. A car pulled up and out shouted a question "Is this where Randy Owen lives?" Without missing a beat, Kelly shouted back, "No, it's not. You go down this road about five miles and across the river. You'll see it up there on the right." I asked her why she had lied and she said, "Do you see what I look like? I'm not gonna have people say they saw me out here chopping wood with my hair in curlers." We both had a good laugh at that one.

While I loved my Alabama boys, I had friendships with many of our other artists as well. Waylon Jennings was a singer with a big voice who recorded for RCA and came to the office quite often. He and Willie Nelson had pioneered the outlaw era in the mid seventies and their antics were the stuff of legends. At that time, most of the desks had name plates on the front, so Shelia Shipley was prominently displayed on the front of mine. The very first time I met Waylon, he stepped off the second floor elevator and began to cross the area to my desk. He saw my name plate and plopped down in the chair in front of me.

"My grandmother was a Shipley," he said. "Is your family from Texas?"

I explained that Shipley was my married name and I didn't think we had any family in Texas. Regardless, Waylon always stopped to talk about the name. He probably mentioned it to me twenty times on his visits. Sometimes, he brought his son Shooter. Shooter was just a baby then, but Waylon let me hold him. Shooter always grabbed my breast and Waylon would laugh and say, "He takes after me." Needless to say, I never told Shooter that he took after his Uncle Tommy either. It must have been a Jennings' thing.

For such a superstar, Waylon always put me at ease, but a lot of the staff was afraid of him. Maybe it was his hell-raising image, but we always got along fine. A couple of times at the Country Radio Seminar, a huge annual gathering of radio people and the country music industry, Joe Galante assigned me to escort Waylon. I was always nervous about it, but I was determined to do my best to take care of and protect him. When I saw Waylon become overwhelmed by the crowds or begin to sweat, I'd move him somewhere quiet to cool down. We never had a problem, and he always seemed to appreciate my efforts to shield him.

Later, when we worked together at MCA, my promotion team gave Waylon his first number one single in ten years with "Rose in Paradise." Due to the chart methodology at that time, a song had to maintain a certain number of points for each area of the chart. These points were garnered by hitting specific benchmarks on radio station playlists.

For example, an add to the playlist from a reporting station picked up five points, then bonus points were picked up each time a song hit a multiple of five from forty to ten on the chart. Forty, thirty-five, thirty, etcetera. If the song went from thirty-six to number thirty-five it picked up a point. Thirty-five to thirty-one got nothing, even though it made a larger move on the chart. From ten to number one, the chart was inverted with number ten garnering one point and number one garnering ten points.

When records lost their bullet (the indication that the single was moving up the charts), due to missing the amount of points necessary to keep it, radio stations often pulled the single from their playlists and a song began to fall. We lost the bullet on "Rose in Paradise" three times but I convinced radio to stick with us. MCA was the first label to ever get a bullet back multiple times and then take the song to number one. That was probably my favorite number one, just because of the extreme effort it took to pull it off. It was also a special gift to Waylon and he never forgot that.

During that time, Waylon toured with his one-man show and I saw him perform acoustically and tell stories at Duke University. That series of shows was incredible. We also booked Waylon to headline the Hoedown Festival in Detroit, and watching him from backstage was one of the highlights of my career.

RCA was home to some incredible talent. Not only did I work with Waylon Jennings, but I got the chance to work with Charley Pride, Eddie Rabbit, Dolly Parton, Jerry Reed, Ronnie Milsap, Eddy Raven, Steve Wariner, Razzy Bailey, Dean Dillon, and many others. During the five years I was at RCA, I got to promote the release of Dolly Parton's *9 to 5* movie and soundtrack, and Jerry Reed's *Smokey and the Bandit* project. It was an incredible opportunity to experience a much bigger world of entertainment than I had experienced at Monument. The RCA staff also took part in the Nashville premiere of both movies. It was a magical time in music and I had a front row seat.

And that's what my job was all about. Music. It is an emotional industry, but for better or for worse, I have always been honest with artists and managers about their music. As Momma taught me, the truth will always come out anyway, so you might as well deliver the bad news as well as the good. Artist and managers also seemed to deal better with the truth if they had the chance to prepare themselves before the chart numbers were announced each week.

Here's an example. About a year before I left RCA, Joe moved one of our branch managers to Nashville and made him vice president of national promotion. The man was feeling his way into the new position, and I'm not sure if he had radio promotion in his background, but he certainly knew sales and marketing from the record distribution level.

At the time, we were working a Dean Dillon single and having a bit of difficulty with it. The new national VP had a conversation either with Dean or his manager several days before the chart was to be posted and told them everything was okay with the single. I knew that wasn't the case, but I also knew better than to contradict or say anything that would throw the new boss under the bus.

When the chart closed out that week, Dean's single lost a bullet and all hell broke loose at RCA. With my desk sitting just outside the elevator door, I got to see all of the comings and goings. About three P.M. the day after the charts came out, the elevator doors opened and Dean Dillon stepped out. With a stagger and a bottle of Jack Daniels Black Label, he proceeded down the hallway toward Joe's office. I never heard what was discussed, but I sure heard that bottle break against the wall. I heard Joe call for the national VP and doors slammed. I guess Dean made his point about getting a legitimate heads up when a song is going down.

In the late 1970s and early 1980s, Nashville could be a fun place. There were a lot of unique characters who enjoyed playing practical jokes on each other. Like many other businesses, the music industry goes through cycles as personalities and leadership change hands. Practical jokes seemed to be part of the personality of several of the creative people who guided careers of that time period. Though it didn't happen often, I did get to experience a prank or two. Jerry Bradley and Tom Collins were two highly competitive pranksters. Jerry Bradley was the president of RCA Nashville and the son of legendary producer Owen Bradley. Tom Collins was a celebrated producer of Barbara Mandrell, Ronnie Milsap, and many others who also ran a very successful music publishing company. Stories abound on those two and an entire book could be written about their pranks, which continued for many years.

Jerry was known to have jacked up Tom's car while he was in the recording studio one night at Javelina Studio. He removed all of the tires while Tom was recording, and left the car up on cement blocks. On another occasion I was getting ready for work only to learn on the TV morning news that someone had dumped a load of horse manure on the steps of the RCA building. What the news didn't reflect, and what I would later find out, was how it got there.

Jerry Bradley, along with a buddy, had loaded a pick up truck with manure and junk, and taken it to Tom Collins's office. Then they piled it on his steps all the way up past the mail slot. They were throwing old tires and other stuff into the mix when drunken neighbors from an apartment building next door began contributing stuff to the pile. Of course, this all took place in the wee hours of the morning, long before daybreak. Someone else called Tom and told him they had seen a truck in front of his office and people dumping crap on his porch. Somehow, Tom found enough friends in the middle of the night to conveniently move said manure to the RCA steps long before daybreak.

There was also the time that Joe Galante rolled the office with toilet tissue after a late night of partying. On another occasion, Joe and some helpers re-arranged Jerry Bradley's office by turning all of the photos and chairs upside down, leaning the couch against the door and crawling out through the door before it slammed shut. The couch was now firmly holding the door shut. When Jerry arrived at the office for his first meeting of the day, he couldn't get the door open and had to push his way into his office. Non-pulsed, Jerry kept his scheduled meeting and met in his office with everything in disarray.

I stayed out of most of the hi-jinks and kept my nose to the grindstone, making it a point to arrive at work early. Most mornings I took Michael to school, and then headed to the office to catch up before everyone else arrived. The next to arrive was usually Jerry Bradley or Joe Galante. One morning, Jerry arrived first and walked through the office with his hands full of phone cords. He had removed the cords from all of our desk phones. This was long before there was such a thing as a cordless phone. Then Jerry grabbed the cord from my desk and told me not to say a word.

Jerry next collected cords from the conference room and from couch tables. His plan was to take them all. Then he was going to have Joe buzzed and told that our New York label president was calling for him. Jerry thought it would drive Joe nuts not to be able to answer that phone. But Joe was hard to catch off guard. He paid attention to detail. Somehow, Joe noticed the missing phone cords and managed to find one downstairs on the first floor. He had that cord in his pocket when the call came through. But, when Joe attached it to the phone to take the call, Jerry stepped in with scissors and cut it in half. The laugh over, the cords were returned and we went about our work. I doubt seriously that anything like that happens today—at least during business hours—but it sure kept everyone on their toes.

There were good days at work and bad. Some days I left work depressed because I felt so worthless and beat down. Maybe I wanted success too badly, or maybe I just wanted respect. I also wanted more from my marriage and felt I had to wear too many hats both personally and in my career. In my marriage, I wanted intimacy. Maybe my expectations were more than any man could give. I wanted our family to be more involved in church, and Bennie to take a stronger role in our family. I also wanted Michael to grow up in the church and become a good man with a solid foundation of faith. I wanted to be a good wife and mother, but I did not want to be wife, mother, brother, sister, and parent to my husband.

As for Michael, he had experienced problems in school from the day he started. In his early years, it was being over active in class or walking outside without permission. We had him tested in the first grade through Metro Nashville Public Schools but the educators said that while Michael was borderline, he did not have Attention Deficit Disorder (ADD). By the time he reached the seventh grade, however, Bennie and I met with an independent psychologist who asked us to retrieve Michael's paperwork from Metro schools and bring it to him.

here, in black and white, we discovered that the person who had tested Michael in the first grade had subtracted wrong. Michael did have ADD and it had been reflected in that early test. We had lost seven years where he could have been treated. By now, Michael was suffering from low self-esteem and running with other kids who were feeling the same way about themselves. We found a school in Williamson County, the county just south of Nashville, that worked with children with ADD. Willow Hall was a private school that only went through the eighth grade so we would have to make other arrangements for high school. I was thrilled when Michael began to excel in their teaching environment.

About that time, Bennie lost his job at WSIX and I was forced to support our family of three on fifteen thousand dollars a year. I debated what to do with my life and struggled with the decision. Maybe it was time to look for something better. Discreetly, I began to put out feelers for another job—or a second job—and waited.

If RCA had offered me more money, a title and an office, I might have stayed because, whether he knew it or not, Joe Galante was my mentor. He was a complex man with a unique way of leading people, and he taught me more about the music business than anyone I have ever worked for. This was partially because Joe was the epitome of vision. He was also a marketing strategist who left nothing to guess work. Joe looked at chart statistics with an eye to other labels performances for the same time period. Then he challenged us to be the best. Joe felt that number one was all that counted, and that number two did not.

While I would one day develop many of the traits I admired in Joe, I also chose not to treat my employees the way we were sometimes treated. I felt that motivation by intimidation is not a long-term plan for success. Once I got the opportunity to lead, I developed my own strategies to motivate personnel.

At RCA I was given praise privately and allowed to attend select functions that involved marketing and promotion when others in the office were not. But on top of all my other issues with RCA I could never break into the inner circle and I decided it was time to move on. I spoke to my immediate boss, Dave Wheeler, and asked why he thought it was so hard for me to move into another position. He shook his head in dismay and said he didn't have a clue. He was sorry.

Five years into my job I realized I would never achieve what others around me had. I loved RCA so much that it was starting to consume me. At the same time, I struggled with my career and resolved myself to the fact that even though I might never be more than an assistant to someone else, it wouldn't be at RCA. I prepared to leave.

About this same time, my old friend John Dorris was starting a new management company to represent the iconic recording artist Don Williams. I had worked with John at Monument and had stayed in touch during my five years at RCA. John asked if I would be interested in interviewing with Don about a position they had, so I scheduled a lunch meeting.

The choice ultimately came down to one other female candidate who had worked for Don's former manager—and me. I thought it was a long shot, but went to lunch with Don Williams to discuss the new position and see what he thought of me. Don apparently liked me, as he offered me the position that very day. The new job was far less work and increased my salary by ten thousand dollars.

"You can't leave the number one company in the business to work for a company that has no identity," Joe said when I turned in my resignation, "You are taking a chance, going to work for a new company that might close its doors in a year."

"That gamble is on me, Joe," I said. "If the company folds, then I'll turn up somewhere else."

"It's going to take three people to replace you, Shelia," he said. "Won't you consider staying? What will it take to keep you here?"

When I told him, he said he'd make a call to the New York office and give me an answer in two hours. Then he asked that I tell no one until he spoke to me again. While I doubted that he would come back with an offer that would satisfy me, I was pleased that he was willing to try.

I honored Joe's wishes and held our conversation private. Joe must have wanted to speak to our national rep about the situation, as they left for lunch not long after our meeting. Within a few hours, I had calls from two friends who had been offered my job: Janet Bozeman worked at a Nashville country reporting station, and Sharon Allen in *R&R*'s sales department. Now, how is it that I am to tell no one of the discussion, yet less than two hours later the national has offered my job to two of my friends? It was not looking good for staying.

That afternoon, Joe called me into his office and informed me that he could get my title changed and give me more money (he didn't say how much), but he could not give me an office. I would still be outside the elevator doors and in addition to my new responsibilities; I would still work for the director of sales. They could not afford to hire a secretary for him that would replace me. After hearing his proposal, I knew it was time to move on. It was November 1983, and several years passed before I told Joe about the phone calls from my friends who were offered my job.

I took the job as director of career coordination for Hallmark Direction Company. For the next four months, I set up files and organized the new office, and I made one road trip to Beaumont, Texas to see Don Williams's show. I also spent a whole lot of time waiting to be given answers or direction on projects and started to feel that my choice in a new job might not have been the right one. I wondered what to do. My work load was one fourth what it had been at RCA. While I made more money, there was no challenge in the work I was doing. I found myself once again growing frustrated, but for very different reasons.

The RCA Promotion Team with Charley Pride and Alabama

With the Judds at the RCA Suite during Country Radio Seminar

Gaylen Adams (RCA), Sylvia, Jerry Reed, my son Michael and Bennie Shipley

at the "Smokey & The Bandit" movie premiere

At the "9 To 5" Movie premiere with Dolly and Mary Ray (RCA)

CHAPTER 8

MCA Records

In February of 1984, when I had been with Hallmark Direction Company for three months, I received a call from Gene Hughes. Gene was one of the few independent promotion reps that Joe had hired to work RCA product, so I saw him often in the RCA offices. Joe was not usually open to independent promoters, but he did allow Gene Hughes to work records for him. I always thought it was because he liked to keep his game plan internal. Since Joe trusted Gene, I felt I could trust him as well.

I had last spoken to Gene about a year before I left RCA, when I was putting out feelers for a new industry position. Now, Gene told me that MCA Records was going through a regime change and everyone at the company was being replaced. A man named Jimmy Bowen was to head up the new operation. Bowen had been in Nashville for several years and most recently had headed up Warner Brothers Records. He was a flamboyant personality who loved to start rumors just as much as music industry people loved to discuss them.

While at Warner, Bowen had made two women vice presidents, which created a flurry of chatter along the streets of Music Row. Prior to moving to Nashville, Bowen had produced hits for Frank Sinatra, Dean Martin, Sammy Davis Jr., and Glen Campbell. He also ran his own label, Amos Records, in Los Angeles from 1968-1971. Once in Nashville, and with a lot of country success with Hank Williams, Jr., he was to sit at the new helm of a country label as its new chief. Gene had been hired as vice president of promotion and wanted to know if I would consider coming to MCA to work with him.

The chance that I might work for MCA was exciting, and it sounded like the position was a radio promotion job. Bowen was to make the final decision and Gene arranged an interview. I met with

Bowen and Hughes that same week upstairs at Sound Stage Studios on Music Row where Bowen kept an office.

This interview was like no other I have had before or since. Although I was prepared to talk about my experience and how I might benefit MCA and its artists, it didn't come up. Bowen did most of the talking, explaining his record business philosophy and what he looked for in personnel. Occasionally he asked me a question, which I answered. He then returned to the subject he was originally talking about.

One of the things he said was that his long-time friend Bruce Hinton was joining MCA as vice president and general manager, and that he was bringing Tony Brown in as a head of A&R. Bruce had done independent record promotion and had worked on the *Urban Cowboy* movie with Jim Ed Norman, who took the helm of Warner Bros. Records when Bowen headed to MCA. Norman was a musician who had played in a band with Don Henley in the seventies. A record with the band was released on Bowen's Amos Records. When the group disbanded, Norman went on to be one of the architects of the Western sound of nineties rock and pop. Bowen, Hinton, and Norman were all friends and actually shared a house in the Los Angeles hills.

I had met Bruce before at industry events, but did not know him well. I knew Tony from my years at RCA, so the pieces were beginning to feel like a fit. By now you've probably figured out that the music industry in Nashville can be a very small place. People bounce around from place to place, often working with the same people numerous times.

"You make me feel comfortable," said Bowen, "and if you make me feel comfortable, you'll make our artists feel comfortable. So, if you want the job, it's yours!"

That was it. He offered me thirty thousand a year, which was twice what I had made at RCA just four months earlier. I started with MCA two weeks later as their manager of promotion.

But, as I walked out the door with Gene, Bowen said, "She'll do great with those retail reporters."

I almost stopped in my tracks. It was then that I realized even though my new title was promotion manager, I had been hired to work the *sales* charts, not the *radio* charts. It was a job I had never done before. Georgeann Galante, who was married to Joe Galante, had handled that at RCA. I understood the theory but had never played the game. Georgeanne also managed Earl Thomas Conley and Razzy Bailey, which kept the circle even smaller. Both artists recorded for RCA.

However, I wasn't about to walk away from a thirty-thousand dollar a year job offer. I believed I could figure sales promotion out the same way I had figured out how to do radio promotion. Bowen was gambling on me and I was not about to let him down. Bowen was the kind of guy who said exactly what he felt and exactly what he expected. He put everything out there on the line, but he seemed fair. Besides, Tony Brown was also coming to MCA along with artists Waylon Jennings and Steve Wariner. All three had been at RCA Records when I was there, and I felt comfort in knowing some of the people I would once again work with.

So in March of 1984, I began my new job at MCA. I was so excited. Not only was MCA a great company, it had incredible artists and we were on the ground floor of writing a new chapter in the company's history as a label.

Promotion teams share a unique bond. Since most of us did not know each other personally, the very first weekend of my new job, we decided to have a promotion retreat for the staff so we could get to know each other better and develop strong relationships. Gene and I had discussed location and I had recommended a resort in Crossville, Tennessee that the RCA staff had attended for meetings on several occasions. I was looking forward to the weekend and getting to know the staff.

The resort was about a two hour drive from Nashville. We rented a ten-passenger van and headed east, toward Knoxville. The team arrived and went to an early dinner at a local restaurant. Most of the time when you have a gathering like this, there are alcoholic beverages and storytelling, as people let down their guard and got to know each other.

But at dinner our first night together, Gene did not allow anyone to order any alcoholic beverage. When the waitress arrived to take our drink order, Gene immediately said no alcohol tonight. You could see the surprised looks from everyone at the table. Their eyes were all asking "what have I gotten into?" Later, we discovered that Gene was a recovering alcoholic, but his problem was now extended to the team of people who were working with him.

When we got back to the resort, Gene turned to everyone and said, "Goodnight. I will see everyone in the morning. Get some rest."

It was barely eight o'clock. There were a few awkward moments as everyone stood there and tried to figure out what to do. I did not know this new team, so I said my goodnights and headed back to my room as well. I later learned that some of the others found a bowling alley and played a few games before returning to the resort.

About eleven-thirty that night, my hotel phone rang. It was Gene.

"I have to talk to you," he said.

"When?" I inquired.

"Now. I am coming over."

I began to tremble, but pulled a robe over my pajamas and waited for his knock on my door. I couldn't imagine what could be so urgent as to require a meeting at that hour of the night. I opened the door and before I could utter a word, Gene pushed in and promptly sat down on the foot of my bed.

"What's wrong?" I asked.

He replied by patting the bed and asking me to sit next to him. I stood there like a deer in the headlights wondering whether to sit, run, or scream. Gene again patted the bed.

"I need someone to hold. Won't you come over and lie next to me?" he asked.

My knees were shaking and my heart was racing. I was asking myself what in the world I had gotten myself into, but I didn't move. I stood like a stone statue praying I would know what to say or how to get away. The seconds seemed like eternity as Gene continued to stare at me. Then Gene, realizing that I was not coming over to champion his needs, raised himself from the bed and left my room without a word.

Door locked, I placed a chair under the doorknob and listened for the sound of footsteps, or a jigger at the lock. Then shivering, I called John Dorris. I described in great detail what had happened and asked what I should do. Sweet man that he is, he offered to drive to Crossville and bring me back to Nashville. I thanked him, but told him I would be okay, as I would not answer the phone or door if he tried to get in again.

I loved my new job and despite the circumstances didn't feel I should quit just yet. I had never been a quitter before. So, I waited for morning with one ear listening for the handle on the door to jiggle. When morning came, I went down to the restaurant where we all met for breakfast. Gene acted as if the midnight visit to my room had never taken place, so I did the same. I decided to hold on to that job and to hold my tongue. I had way too much to lose. We had a few days of productive meetings at the resort, then the weekend was over and everyone traveled back to Nashville together before going their separate ways.

When I returned to Nashville, I settled into my new responsibilities. Mainly, I called retail stores to promote album reports. These reports set the chart numbers for the *Billboard* Country Album Chart. This chart was compiled pre-SoundScan, so sales reports were garnered much in the way of record promotion. My goal was to use my relationship with the retailer to get my George Strait album to report as the number one seller in a particular week. That way we could debut at a higher position than our competition. It was very much like radio promotion and sometimes the retailer would do a "gimme" for one week to assist me in obtaining my goal.

Within four months of joining MCA Nashville, I debuted George Strait's "Ocean Front Property" as the number one album––the first time it had ever been done in country. When all the numbers were tallied and the news was announced, I had pulled it off. It was a first for me *and* a first for George Strait! That was a proud day for me and a huge accomplishment. I still have the framed letter that Strait's manager, Erv Woolsey, sent to me congratulating me on the feat. By year end, MCA was named the Album Label of the Year by *Billboard,* taking the honor away from the industry leader, my old alma mater, RCA Nashville.

In addition to my sales report responsibilities, I assisted the promotion department. Gene Hughes was the vice president of promotion and Patti Olsen was the national director. Patti had joined Gene's independent promotion company about a year before joining MCA. While she later held a similar position at Mercury Records before starting her own independent promotion team, she did not appear to have a lot of experience in calling radio at this time. Instead, she seemed to defer to Gene on the decision making.

I found out that most of the original MCA staff had been hired under the Erv Woolsey regime. Erv had left MCA to become George Strait's manager, a much more secure position than the job he had at MCA. Because the new staff was part of a new regime, I worried that the regionals would have a loyalty to Woolsey, and be uncomfortable with the new leadership. I could see that the regionals were being misdirected by Gene and getting more confused with each passing week. With mounting frustration, they began to open up and trust me with their fears and questions.

For example, they were told to get commitments for airplay at specific stations, which was impossible. You can't call a regional up and say "this week, I want you to get WKHX-Atlanta, WCOS-Charlotte, WKIS-Miami, and WQDR-Raleigh to add Steve Wariner." You had to ask them about their conversations with programmers, determine who liked the single best, and who was closest to adding the song. That would make those who liked the song a target for the week. Throwing out a broad net without knowing if there are any fish in the water ends up with nothing caught.

Frustrated, the regionals often called me to ask what they should do.

"Essentially, the label is asking you to get four adds on Steve Wariner," I told them. "It may not be the specific four they are asking for, but try to get four adds. Go for the stations that will add the song. The results will be the same."

Even though my duties were to work the retail chart, as part of the promotion team I did my best to help the regionals navigate through the new leadership maze. So, I guided the regional reps with the same direction as I did at RCA, only this time it was me who was actually guiding, not me just feeding Joe Galante info to the team. I encouraged our team and praised them when they called in adds. Over a period of months, the team began to depend on me and called more often for advice. We were having success and I was a large part of that. Being able to take what I had learned and apply it without someone telling me what to do—and being successful in the process—was rewarding.

While the regionals had issues with their vice president of promotion, I had my own problems with Gene Hughes beyond what I experienced that night in Crossville. As I had done at RCA, I wrote weekly reports recapping what had happened in my world, and copied Gene, Bowen, and Bruce Hinton. This was back in the days when you typed memos and circulated them to all of the parties by placing the reports in each person's mail tray. As everyone arrived for work, or came back from lunch, they walked through the mailroom to pick up mail and memos.

At one point Gene was questioned about something I had summarized in a report. He had not taken the time to read my report and was caught off guard. This really set him off. He marched into my office and insisted I give him *all* the copies of my report from that moment forward, and he would circulate them. I knew no one would ever see them after that. The regionals expense reports were piled on his desk, and instead of reviewing, approving, and passing them on for reimbursement, Gene let them sit for weeks at a time. At one point, I found out that the staff had gone almost four months without being reimbursed. This was certainly no way to run a business, and it was a miserable time for everyone involved.

Gene's harassment became harder for me. Maybe it was because I shunned Gene's advances. Maybe it was because Gene wanted more control over the "women" in his life. He pushed every button possible with me and I was secretly more miserable than I had ever been in my life. I wasn't allowed to leave the building for lunch. Gene refused to have me out of his sight and told me that I needed to eat at my desk. I had to order lunch in, and ninety-nine percent of the time Gene would walk past my desk, pick up my sandwich and take a bite out of it, or eat something else off my plate.

One time I was called at eleven-thirty in the evening, awakened by Gene,

"Meet me in the office at seven A.M." he said.

"What's wrong?" I asked.

"Just be there."

I showed up at six-forty-five and Gene didn't stroll in until nine. He acted as if he knew nothing about a meeting. This scenario happened over and over again. I was cursed at and threatened, and it all made me feel as if I was in prison and Gene was the warden.

Regardless, I kept my head down and continued to do my job; I was not going to be driven away, especially because I had no place else to go. I know I can be a bit gullible. I usually take people at face value and believe what they tell me, until I discover otherwise. A month or so into the job, I realized that Gene and Patti had a personal relationship. Clueless me had no idea they were living together. They came to work in separate cars. They left at different times. They were friendly, but I had no idea just how friendly.

It turned out that Patti felt threatened, too. It's no wonder that she carried out Gene's directions, she was afraid of losing her job—and her way of life. On numerous occasions Gene suggested I spend the weekend on his boat with the two of them. Of course, there was no way I was sleeping on a boat with Gene and Patti. First, I can't swim and it is a long way from shore when someone asks you to do something you choose not to do. Second, I didn't want to be a *Billboard* headline for being mysteriously lost in Old Hickory Lake. Still, the innuendos and threats continued.

One morning Patti and I were called into Gene's office. Gene sat behind his desk and his face was blood red. He stood up and the veins in his neck stood out as he called us every horrible, vulgar, and demeaning name imaginable. Gene said he would "fire us both." He told Patti that he pulled her out of the gutter and he would drive her back there. Then he threatened to strip Patti of her credit cards and drive her into bankruptcy. He was not going to tolerate our insubordination.

Since I had not been insubordinate, I determined then and there that I would take no more. Shaking, I followed Patti back into her office.

"You may live with him and love him and allow him to speak to you that way," I said. "And as long as I work here I will tolerate him. I will not cause him trouble or go over his head, but I will never lie for him, if asked. Understand that. I will not cover for his insanity or his ravings or you making excuses for him because of his alcoholism. I will not be his toy nor his plaything. I am done with Gene Hughes. I have no respect for that man and he has lost my friendship."

I may not have liked Gene, but one thing I liked a lot about Jimmy Bowen was that he always stayed in direct touch with the regionals. He wanted to hear what radio was saying about our music. So, he asked that each of the regionals call him over the weekend to discuss the week past—what they had heard, what they had been up to, what the competition was doing. It was also a way for the regional reps to check up on the home office during those first few months, so I am sure they confided much in Bowen's ears. Trust me, he had a way of pulling information out of you.

Bowen also listened to Pat Schoffstoll, who was his office manager and head of personnel. Her office was next to mine and she had overhead several of Gene's rants, including the morning he exploded over my visiting our new office space and checking out furniture for a move the label would soon make. Bowen wasn't in the office a lot. I saw him in the weekly staff meeting but rarely had a one-on-one conversation with him outside those meetings.

One evening around nine o'clock, however, I received a call from Bowen. He caught me off guard when he simply said, "Talk to me."

"What about?" I asked.

"Gene Hughes didn't hire you and he cannot fire you," Bowen said.

I got the message. I realized that Gene had tried to rid himself of the independent free-thinking female he had working for him. Even though I was the one making him look good, he still felt threatened. No doubt about it, Gene was out to do me in.

Before I could say more, Bowen went on to tell me what he already knew, and it was far more than I ever imagined. Pat had told him about the harassment and the threats. Bowen knew the regionals' expense reports had not been turned in for four months, and that they were found stacked on Gene's desk. In addition, Bowen said that disturbing comments had been heard by some big ears in the office. Whether it was true or not, he told me he had the office bugged. He knew what Gene was telling people behind his back.

"You have never lied to me, Shelia," he said. "You tell the same story no matter who is listening."

That evening, Bowen let me know that he was firing Gene Hughes. Bowen had a bad mouth on him and loved to throw out colorful, unsettling words. He even called Patti names in our staff meeting in front of the entire staff. He went on to say that Patti would be taking over the department until he could figure something out, "but after that the 'red headed wench' will be gone."

Part of me was ecstatic, but another part of me was very sad. Someone I had once known and trusted had destroyed the best chance he ever had to achieve success and notoriety at a major record label. He had thrown it all away with petty jealously, and by not taking care of the business at hand. Maybe he was in over his head. Regardless, his days at MCA were numbered and a major change was about to blow through the label.

The next morning it was announced that Gene Hughes was no longer with the company. He had lasted exactly six months. It was also announced that Patti Olsen was running promotion in the interim. That was September and by late November, the tide had changed again. Bowen fired Patti Olsen and installed me as the temporary chief. I was honored to be temporarily in charge, but I was also frightened at the huge responsibility that had fallen on my shoulders. Before I could utter any concern, however, Bowen spit out his plan.

"We'll let everyone think it is Bruce who is running the show, so don't feel any pressure," said Bowen. "If we lose all the bullets on the chart, we'll tell everyone 'Bruce did it.'"

Even though the job was a hot seat, I filled in. I directed the regionals and planned the strategies every week. I directed them the way I had directed the RCA reps (although there I had Joe Galante telling me what to do).

David Haley was hired a few months before Gene and Patti left the building. He had been in radio in Jackson, Mississippi before moving to Nashville and had known both of them for a few years. I was never sure what David was hired to do, but I liked him a lot. Patti had him running errands and painting her office. Occasionally, I saw him on the phone. Now that I was calling the shots I thought it best to determine what his job description was supposed to be.

One day I called David into my office to determine a better way to utilize his talent. I wanted him on the phones calling radio. Since the regionals were calling all of the major market reporters in their assigned territories, I decided we could start him calling the *R&R* reporting stations, which at that time were considered secondary to the major markets. It was still airplay and as I have always said, "All airplay is good airplay." We developed a region for David and he hit the phones. Then Bowen did something amazing. Each December, Bowen headed to Hawaii for an extended vacation. He was usually gone three to four weeks. This time, before he left, he called me.

"I'm going on vacation and am leaving you in charge," he said. "You have never let me down and you won't now. I trust you. But, I also want you to know something. I don't give a damn about bullets on the chart. I'm here to sell records. If we lose every bullet while I am gone, you still have a job with me when I get back. You're too good to lose. So don't worry. Take care of our music and our music will take care of you."

I had never been so afraid in my life. Bowen empowered me to lead. No one in the industry knew that I was making the decisions; they thought my boss, Bruce Hinton, was calling the promotion shots. After all, Bruce was a promotion veteran so it made sense that he could supervise and direct the staff. Bowen, however, told Bruce to shield me from the outside during that time.

When Bowen returned a month later, MCA had the highest charting singles on *Billboard* and *R&R* every week he was gone. MCA had celebrated two consecutive #1 singles, one from George Strait, "Does Fort Worth Ever Cross Your Mind," and Reba McEntire's third number one (and first for MCA), "How Blue." We had not lost a single record. As a matter of fact, by the end of 1984 we had celebrated twelve number one singles, and held that coveted number one spot for seventeen out of fifty-two weeks. It was an unprecedented accomplishment for a single label.

Even with the chart success we had experienced as a team, Hinton and Bowen continued interviewing for the new vice president of promotion. After all, I was just a fill-in, juggling two jobs just as I had at RCA. Why should they consider me for the position? Why should I ask to be considered? They interviewed men from pop promotion, country promotion, and various radio fields. It was a Who's Who that marched through the hallway in an effort to impress and capture the coveted leadership position.

One day Bruce Hinton came into my office and sat down across from me. He asked how I felt about the job now that I had been handling it for six months. I said I enjoyed it, but would be glad when a decision was finally made. He looked at me oddly, then asked if I would consider the job. I was stunned. Had I heard him correctly? Even though I desperately wanted the position, I asked why he considered me for the job. Women were not holding key leadership positions in the industry, and none were in head of promotion positions. Regionals would take a lot of heat working for a woman, and that the company wouldn't want that image either. After all, that is what I had always been told, when I was slapped back whenever I asked for consideration before.

As Bruce often did, he made me answer my own question. He asked if I preferred to work with radio or retail.

"Radio."

He then asked if I planned to work the rest of my life.

"Yes," I said.

"Well, if you have to work the rest of your life, wouldn't you rather do something that makes you happy?"

That made perfect sense to me.

Bruce then said, "Based on that, haven't you answered my question? I'll call Bowen and let him know you'll take the job." He also said that each of the regionals had individually spoken to him and to Bowen and asked that I be given the position.

I was stunned. That was a huge turning point for me. Two of the regionals were older than I was and had ten years more experience. If these men were willing to take the chance on me as their leader, then I would never let them down. I was once again at a career crossroad. That one decision changed my life for the next fifteen years. It was to be a roller coaster ride of stress and success, and the best years of my life.

Bowen called me later that day, after Bruce told him of my decision. I told him I was afraid of ridicule from my peers, radio, and the industry. The last thing I wanted was to be joked about.

"When you're good, everybody talks," he said. "The more success you have, the greater the jealousy and the more people talk. Look at what they say about me. Half of it is true and half of it isn't. You can't worry about what other people think. The promotion team wants you to take the job. They believe you can handle it. I believe you can handle it and Bruce does, too."

Decision made. I was the new director of national promotion for MCA Records. Upon hearing the official news, I put my head down and prayed that God would grant me the wisdom and strength to lead my team into a new era. And He did. We would go on to set records and establish practices that would become new standards in our industry.

With Bill Catino, Glen Campbell, and Bruce Hinton at the premier of the *Big River* play in Cleveland, OH

With Reba McEntire during Country Radio Seminar

With Mark Chesnutt, Al Teller, Kelly Willis, and Scott Borchetta

CHAPTER 9

Building My A-Team

Now that I had officially taken over leadership duties for the department, I needed to hire a personal assistant. I wanted someone with experience, a person who wasn't going to have an attitude about digging in and getting the job done. I needed someone who would work as hard as I did, and not whine about it.

I had been interviewing for days and was having no luck in finding the person I felt would complement my personality. The person I was looking for needed to be organized and capable of handling a lot of details. I was in my corner office in the White Hall Building on West End wondering if I could find the person I needed. I became more discouraged as the day wore on, but I had one final interview late in the day with a young woman named Lori Evans.

The minute I met Lori, I liked her. She had worked as an event planner with Patsy Bruce and seemed to be willing to get any job done. Patsy had been married to recording artist, songwriter, and actor, Ed Bruce before she started her company. A great deal of what Lori did with event planning could easily be transferred to organizing showcases or radio events during conventions. She knew how to budget live performance venues, and had booked travel and worked with hotel sales personnel, and catering. After about an hour together, I ushered her from the room and told her I would let her know about the job within a day or two. Deep down I wanted to hire her, but I had one last interview to complete the next morning.

J. L. Allison worked in our mailroom and also performed janitorial services for MCA. He had been with the company for years, and was one of two people to survive the regime change. The other had been Katie Gillon, who would go on to become vice president of creative services.

Katie had been with ABC and Dot Records before it was merged with MCA. Prior to us joining the company, she was Jim

Foglesong's executive assistant and was already handling much of the same paperwork and clearances she did now with the new regime. Creative services is the area of a label that handles photo sessions, retouching, artwork for albums, and clearances for the label copy used in the booklets or covers. Katie was a brilliant woman and Bowen was smart to retain her. She also definitely knew how to navigate the MCA system to get records out.

Foglesong was a producer and great A&R talent. He had been president of Dot, ABC, MCA, and Capitol, and had signed some of the biggest talent in country music to label deals including Barbara Mandrell, The Oak Ridge Boys, George Strait, Reba McEntire, Garth Brooks, and many others. He was inducted into the Country Music Hall of Fame in 2004.

That night, J.L. was making the rounds of picking up trash before my interview with Lori Evans was over. After she left he passed my door several times before he headed into my office.

"You're gonna hire her, ain't you?" he asked.

"I don't know yet," I said.

"Yes, you are."

"Why do you say that?"

"Because you would just talk, talk, talk, and she would just write, write, write and that's what you need. Someone who will listen to you and do what you say."

He was right. Lori was exactly who I needed. While I did have one last applicant interview the next day, the decision had already been made in my mind. Soon after completing my final interview the next morning, I called Lori back into my office and offered her the job.

Lori is, admittedly, a free spirit. Before she worked with me, she had never stayed in one job longer than eighteen months. She offered that tidbit to me during the interview. I saw something in her, though, and that idle threat didn't scare me. I knew I was stronger than that. Plus, she had never worked for me.

The greatest asset Lori possessed was that I trusted her, and trust is a big thing for me. I don't want my personal or professional information being given out to anyone. Not that I have secrets, but I want someone who has integrity and will have my back during difficult times. Lori was that person.

Lori had worked for Waylon Jennings in the mid 1970s during a time when he was utilizing many non-prescription drugs—among other things. Everyone in Nashville knew what he was doing. Often, walking up the sidewalk to his office, people found pills scattered along the edges of the sidewalk. Lori was very young when she worked for Waylon. Once, she was directed to go to the Nashville airport to pick up a package, and then deliver it to Waylon at the studio where he was recording. She did as directed. Just as she entered the studio, however, one of the engineers looked up and saw federal agents ringing the bell for access.

"Quick. Get rid of the package!" the engineer called.

It was removed from sight and who knows where it went. The agents took Lori into custody and berated her to tell them what was in the package and where it came from. She, of course, had no idea what was in the package, and had nothing to tell. Whether she knew more or not, she never disclosed a thing, and I respected her strong will. Few women her age would have withstood such intense questioning from federal agents.

If you ever watched the television show *M*A*S*H*, then you remember the relationship between the colonel and Radar, the intuitive supply clerk. Lori was my Radar. I don't know how she did it, but we were always on the same wavelength. Our offices were next to each other. Often, when I got up to tell her something, she was already heading toward me and we'd meet in my doorway. Then we'd laugh because we had a similar idea or question about the same topic.

Lori could handle everything I threw at her, and more. I never had another assistant who could juggle as much work as she did. Lori is actually the person who taught me to use a word processor. Before that I used an old Selectric II typewriter, but one evening she set me down and showed me how a word processor worked. I was hooked, and have been ever since. I have worn out many keyboards since that first lesson so many years ago, and will always be thankful for her tutorage and friendship.

Lori's job was to compile our tracking sheets, handle promotional record requests, process concert ticket buys, book travel for the staff, artists, and me; plan conventions and events; and always stay a step ahead of my needs and me. She was always there for me and I treasure her friendship.

While I was at RCA, we had been involved in the release of two movies, *9 to 5* and *Smokey and the Bandit*. At MCA I would get the pleasure of working with film companies to promote four more movies *Sweet Dreams* (1985), *Pure Country* starring George Strait (1992), *8 Seconds to Glory* starring Luke Perry (1994), and Black Dog starring Patrick Swayze (1998). Creating radio promotions, movie premieres, and screenings to promote these films was huge for our country stations, and further solidified the relationship we held between promotion personnel and radio programmers.

MCA had the soundtracks to these projects, and the combination of our efforts in creating radio promotions was a win-win for us in sales, and for the film company in creating awareness for the movie releases. Often, we worked single tracks from these soundtracks in an effort to chart songs that were featured in the films.

I loved my promotion team. I truly mean that. Maybe guys don't think that way or say that, but I truly loved my guys (girls included). Joe Deters lived in Atlanta and was our Southeast rep. Joe was like a father figure to me. Each year on his birthday, when I asked how old he was, he always seemed to be the "double-nickel" meaning fifty-five years old. It took me a few years to catch on, but Joe never aged. I never knew how old he really was, nor did I care. He had the energy of a much younger man and his passion for music was undeniable. Joe could definitely hear a hit song and was always right on target with his single picks.

Joe has since passed away, but never a day goes by that I don't think of him. As a radio promoter, I was involved in a tremendous amount of travel. Sometimes, I visited key personnel at their radio station, and other times I escorted them to a concert or an event in their market. Joe taught me to pace myself on the road, and not tire or run out of energy before the day was up. He was also my protector. If a radio programmer had too much to drink and began to make a pass at me, I often slipped away to the other side of the room, or wrapped it up and headed to my room if the evening was coming to an end. Joe also talked a mile a minute. It was often irritating to those around him but I never minded his stories or his words of wisdom.

Early in my role as the head of promotion, Joe and I were traveling through the Carolinas and one of our stops was to cover a show at WTQR in Winston-Salem. Steve Wariner and Reba McEntire were performing on that outdoor show. Since both were MCA artists, we made that city our last visit so we could cover the show. When our recording artists traveled through a city that had a reporting station in it, the regional and/or national rep often attended the event and facilitated the backstage area as a meet and greet for radio.

This was the last leg of our road trip, and this particular concert was an afternoon show. Since we had been on the road all week, we had not planned to stay until the end of the show. Joe and I both had flights out that evening to return home.

It was a multi-artist show so we arrived early to visit with our artists. We got on Steve Wariner's bus and visited with him and his tour manager, T.K. Kimbrell. Then, we stood outside in the sun and watched Steve's performance. It was a blistering hot summer day and we were desperate to get out of the sun for a few minutes while we waited for our headliner, Reba McEntire, to perform.

Finally, Joe told me he was going over to Reba's bus to see if we could come by early for a visit. As soon as we accomplished that, we could head to the airport and enjoy the air conditioning of the car. Several times Joe went to Reba's bus and each time he returned a few minutes later. "It's going be a while longer," He'd say. We stood out in the sun waiting . . . and waiting. The day got later and later and hotter and hotter. I told Joe I didn't want Reba to feel pressed to see us, and certainly didn't want to go on the bus just minutes before she was to perform. After all, most artists have a fifteen to thirty minute ritual prior to a show to prepare themselves mentally to go on the stage. That was not a time when I wanted to interrupt for a visit.

Another hour passed and once again, Joe went to Reba's bus to speak to Narvel Blackstock, her tour manager at the time, and now her husband and manager. At last Joe returned and said it was time, and we boarded her bus to pay our respects to Reba before heading to the airport. We only had about ten minutes before she had to head to the stage. As we entered the bus, I was in front of Joe. As I started to say hello, Reba looked at Narvel and said, "Shelia Shipley, I didn't know you were here."

Narvel looked a little pale and began to apologize. I later found out that Narvel thought Joe was there with his daughter, and had deliberately delayed the visit thinking that Joe would stay all afternoon and talk too much. You could see the heat rising with Reba as she realized her vice president of promotion had been standing in the sun all afternoon waiting to see her, and now it was time for her to head to the stage and for us to head to the airport. I am sure it took her a long time to forget that story. Needless to say, I was never denied entrance after that. It remains one of my favorite stories of traveling with Joe.

Joe was from Cincinnati, Ohio and he loved Skyline Chili. He talked about it all the time. Although he had the southeast as his territory, we let him keep Cincinnati for a long time because he loved to go home to get some Skyline.

The first time Joe and I visited Duke Hamilton, the music director and on-air personality at WUBE, a radio station in Cincinnati, Joe made sure we went to his favorite place. Joe explained all the ways you could get it and that this chili wasn't like Texas chili. Both the taste and the experience were far different. I chose a five-way combo: spaghetti, chili, cheese, beans, and onions. Joe was so excited that I chose that particular dish. He was like a proud papa. While others might not like the taste, I loved it, and do to this day. Besides, how can I not? It was Joe's favorite.

Later, we included Cincinnati in Bill Catino's territory. Bill had worked at Columbia Records, and at rock star Meat Loaf's independent label out of Cleveland. Gene Hughes hired him to handle the northeastern region for MCA, and he was based in our Cleveland sales office. About six months after Bill was hired, Gene Hughes was fired. With no Cincinnati trips in his near future, Joe figured out that Kroger could custom order Skyline Chili for him and ship it to his Atlanta location for pickup. He called to let me know my Kroger would do the same for me. He was so excited with the news. You'd think he was calling in an add on a record!

Roger Ramsey Corkill was my Southwest rep and is still a dear friend. "Roger Dodger" was an old rock 'n roll DJ and was working for MCA before I got there. Remembering my run-ins with Wayne Edwards, who had handled the Southwest for RCA and who always tried to get me fired, I was a little concerned about how well Roger would accept me. But Roger accepted me right from the beginning. As a matter of fact, Roger, who was what you might call a character, defended me on more than one occasion.

On our weekly conference calls, we always ran down the confirmations for the next report date song-by-song, and Roger would reel off at least thirty stations that were playing our major stars, such as Reba, Vince Gill, and George Strait—especially George Strait. After all, it would be down-right communistic not to add a new George Strait song right out-of-the-box if you were a Texas reporter, and about thirty of Roger's stations were in Texas.

Some of the other regionals would glare and say, "He can't possibly have all those stations confirmed already." But on report day, they were there. Roger once again led the way.

In 1986, MCA planned a huge George Strait event at the Carlton Dinner Theater in Minneapolis to show all of the programmers what it was like to attend a George Strait concert. The rooms and travel had been booked, and we were to head in that weekend for the event. I was usually at the office by eight-thirty each morning. That Thursday morning, my private line rang and when I answered it, Roger was on the phone. By the tone of his voice, I knew something was terribly wrong.

"Boss Lady," said Roger. "I got some bad news. George Strait's thirteen-year-old daughter, Jennifer, was killed last night in a car accident."

I sat down. Tears filled my eyes as I tried to imagine the pain that George and his wife Norma must be feeling. Roger said the AP Wire Services would be hitting with the news momentarily, and he wanted me to let the staff know. I called Bruce Hinton and Tony Brown first. Then I began to call the regionals so they could notify all of the programmers we had invited for the weekend's event to cancel their travel. It was a sad morning as we gathered, and staff and friends began to hear the news. It would be a long period of healing, and one that George Strait never discussed with the media.

When enough time had passed and Strait was once again touring, we re-scheduled the Carlton Dinner Theater and flew in all of the programmers from the previous guest list. George had already celebrated several number one singles by this time, but many of our Mid-west, West Coast, and Northeast programmers could not understand what was so cool about this Texas troubadour. At the event, tables for each regional's radio stations were grouped together. An MCA regional and/or a staff person sat at each table to attend to the needs of our guests. Afterward, a wonderful reception was planned backstage in the green room.

Long ago, I had asked Roger to never embarrass me in front of radio personnel, or do anything that would jeopardize the trust I placed in him. David Haley was usually his roommate when everyone had to double up, and David was always the one I leaned on when matters with Roger got out of hand.

That night in Minneapolis, shortly before the show began, I looked around and saw all of my staff attending to their duties—all but one. Roger Dodger was missing in action and was nowhere to be found. About that time, the lights went down, the show kicked off, and the announcer said, "Ladies and gentleman, please make welcome, Mr. George Strait."

My eyes continued to search the room. I finally looked up at the stage and that is when I saw him. Standing stage left in the back was Roger Corkill. He was weaving back and forth, and acting like a proud papa. I couldn't get to him during the show so I decided I would deal with him afterward, when we moved from the theater to the green room.

When the show concluded my staff began to usher our radio and retail guests to the green room. Everyone had a beverage and was awaiting the arrival of the King of Country Music. I asked the other regionals if they had seen Roger, and they had not. A few moments later, the door burst open and in a loud voice Roger declared, "Make welcome the King of Country Music, Mr. George Strait." Roger continued to speak in an overly loud voice as I walked to him, then I took hold of his arm and nudged him to be still. Just then, George entered the room and began to mingle with our radio and retail guests.

Trying not to bring more attention to the situation, I whispered to Roger be quiet. At this point, Roger dropped to his knees and locked his arms around my knees extolling how this "is the proudest night of my life," It was not my proudest night of *my* life, however, as two of my regionals, David Haley and Larry Hughes, came to my rescue. With a regional under each arm, Roger was ushered out of the room and into a quiet holding spot while our guests spent time with George Strait.

There is more. When the event concluded, it was time to escort our guests to the buses that were going to transport them to the hotel. It was bitterly cold outside, snow was falling and a chilling breeze about cut me in half. The ground was getting whiter by the minute and we were all hoping we could get to the hotel before the roads became too bad. Programmers were calling out for us to get on board, but I had Roger in tow with David and Bill Catino supporting him under each arm. We told them we would take the next bus.

Everyone, however, wanted to see what the boss lady was going to do to Roger. All our radio friends peered out the bus window awaiting our next move. We sent the first bus on and waited for the second. Finally, we managed to board a bus and head toward the hotel. I so hoped that our guests would be secure in the bar or in their rooms for the evening by the time we arrived at the hotel. The bus trip took longer than usual because snow continued to fall heavily.

Finally, we arrived at the hotel and I quickly saw that the hotel lobby was filled to capacity with our radio guests. It appeared they had waited for us to see what would happen when we arrived. We moved toward the elevators with Bill and David on either side of Roger as we all lumbered toward the elevator. Several programmers wanted to get on the elevator with us, but we suggested they take the next one. When we reached the floor of Roger's room, I reminded him of his promise never to embarrass me. I told him he had let me down and hurt me deeply. With "I'm sorry" rolling off his lips, we turned down the cover and gently put him to bed amid his promises not to leave the room.

On other occasions, when Roger had a scotch too many, I got a middle of the night phone call with the question, "Are you naked?" My reply always was, "Go to sleep." We later figured out that Roger only did this with the people he felt closest to. Aside from the occasional misstep, Roger was a great promotion man and a good friend.

Larry Hughes handled the West Coast. Larry's father had managed Patsy Cline so he had a heritage rich in country music. One of Larry's first jobs was selling merchandise on the Kenny

Roger's tour, so he brought a full mixture of experience to his promotion job. Larry was wiry and strong, and loved to snow ski. I loved the fact that he always treated his territory as if it was his own, personal business, and he was extremely conscientious of the money he spent. I wish more regionals adhered to his work ethic. Larry was diligent and extremely good with detail. It was funny how each of the regionals were so well suited for the areas in which they lived and promoted.

Whenever I traveled with Larry, he always took me somewhere new to eat. He liked trying different kinds of food, and challenged me to be more open minded about my choices. He was actually the first person who got me to try sushi. He was also the first to take me to eat Thai food, and through him I learned the differences between the seasonings and flavors used, as compared to other oriental dishes.

My favorite road trip with Larry was a trip we planned to showcase Kelly Willis. Kelly has often been called "alternative country," or referred to as a new traditionalist. Playing the honky tonks in Texas, she caught the attention of singer songwriter Nancy Griffith (also signed to MCA). Nancy introduced Kelly to Tony Brown who signed her to the label. We decided that it would be cool to spend the day skiing in Salt Lake City and then end up in a hotel suite that evening where Kelly would perform acoustically. It was an intimate setting with ten to fifteen radio guests from the western states. After a day in the snow and a hot bath, everyone was ready to gather for some cocktails, dinner, and some sweet country music from a beautiful, demure artist. It was here at this showcase that I met Denise Roberts for the first time. Little did I know that she would one day work for me and become a dear friend. At the time, she was the music director of KZLA in Los Angeles. We later hired her to do regional promotion at MCA.

Even though I got along with most of the regionals from the get go, Bill Catino and I got off to a rocky start. He often went around me to Bruce Hinton to ask questions, rather than ask me. After we had a strong discussion about chain of command, he and I went on to establish one of the closest relationships I had with my staff. Bill was the epitome of Italian, and family and friends were especially important to him. He had grown up in Cleveland and was proud of his hometown. As we traveled through his territory, I was exposed to some beautiful, historic parts of our country.

Bowen often told us that we worked hard and should take advantage of our travels to see the cities we were in. Often, if we had a couple of hours to kill between appointments, Bill would do just that. After our calls were finished, he'd take me to see an area of a city that was unique. In addition to our radio visits, I got to see the crack in the Liberty Bell, the place where Mother Goose was buried, and where Paul Revere lived. Once we did a Reba dinner show on a boat in the Boston Harbor. On other occasions, we entertained radio guests in New York City and ate in Little Italy. Bill taught me a lot about the finer things in life, including beautiful rugs, crystal, and china.

I came to love all of Bill's family, including his wife, Linda. I met his grandmother, who barely spoke English and still made homemade pasta, rolling it out on a floured cloth to dry on the dining room table. Bill's son, Jimmy, and my son, Michael, are about the same age, and the Catinos became my extended family. Jim is now head of A&R for Sony Nashville.

One of the quirky things that I remember about Bill was his multi-colored tracking system. Before computers, everyone did tracking by hand so Bill had multi-colored pens that he carried in his brief case to notate different things on his tracking sheets. His sheets always looked like rainbow paintings, but he knew exactly what each color stood for, and he knew how to deliver a record. While everyone has a cell phone today, in those days we often had to pull off at a restaurant or look for a roadside phone so the regionals could make their promotion calls. We were all about road maps and roadside phones when traveling. Today, we have cell phones and GPS to guide our way. It's amazing how things have changed.

As I mentioned earlier, when I first met David Haley, he had been hired to be Patti Olsen's assistant and to call on radio. Patti told me that David had once been a preacher and I heard others jokingly call him Reverend Haley. I couldn't figure out why a preacher would want to do record promotion. I knew he had been in radio in Jackson, Mississippi, but couldn't quite get an angle on the preacher thing. I also never could figure out what actually he did—until after I took over the reins of the department.

When I called David in to discuss his job, we began to plan how I could best use him. When I asked him about being a preacher, he laughed out loud and wanted to know where I had heard that. I told him and he laughed again. "No truth to that," he said. It had always been a joke.

I put David on the *R&R* reporting stations as a regional in training. David came out of radio, but he could have been a stand-up comedian. On several occasions over the next few years, I utilized him whenever we had a crowd and needed entertaining. I don't think anyone can meet David Haley and not like him. He has that kind of personality.

When we moved the MCA offices to our location on South Street, just off Music Row, we were in a building that had an open atrium. In that atrium we created a cubicle to house a combination promotion coordinator and promotion receptionist. Pat Payne was hired to fill the job, and had worked at Columbia Records prior to coming to MCA. As was my style, I liked to hear what my staff felt about the new music we were about to promote. One morning early, Pat and I were in the office alone. I called her into my office to ask about a project we were about to release. I asked what songs she liked.

Taken aback, she said, "You're asking me?"

"Of course I'm asking you."

Pat said she wanted to listen again and give me an answer the next day, and true to her word she came back the next morning with her list.

"No one has ever asked my opinion," she said. "Thank you."

I thought it strange that executives have such wonderful opportunities to do their own market research right there in-house and never take advantage of it. I believe that the greatest words spoken to another can be "what do you think?" but only if you then listen, really listen. You might be surprised by the answer.

In the Bowen years, we all had private phones in our office, and Bowen used those to call us directly. He never called through the switchboard. So when the Bowen hotline rang, we knew to jump. Many nights when we were working late, the direct line that sat next to Pat Payne rang. It was always a wrong number. David Haley sat across from Pat and always ran out of his office to answer her line in a sweet, feminine voice. "Beauty Box," he'd say. Sometime he played the role of a hairdresser. Other times, depending on the accent of the person calling, he became a federal agent who asked about their paperwork. He told them he would be over in a minute and they better have all their documents spread out on the coffee table. We'd all stand around, laughing in stitches, as David became the alter ego to whoever was on the end of that wrong-number line.

One of my favorite David Haley stories is the Orange Bazooka. David never drank alcohol. He said it always depressed him, so he never drank. When he was in college, he apparently spent a memorable weekend in New Orleans. On that particular youthful weekend, he had a few too many Hurricanes. David had an early college class and was driving to school on Monday morning following his Hurricane weekend. Running late, he didn't have time for breakfast so he opted for a large glass of orange juice. He was driving along the road toward school and came to a stoplight.

About that time, David had the urge to cough. He coughed a couple of times and then all of a sudden he delivered an Orange Bazooka all over the windshield in front of him. Horns began to honk as the light changed, but he couldn't move his car. Windshield wipers were no use, since the explosion was on the inside. As he began to tell how he had to wipe the windshield with his hands, we all began to giggle and gag at the same time.

A few years ago David suffered a stroke and decided to retire, moving back to his home state of Mississippi. Several of us planned a retirement party for him at Winner's Bar and Grill on Division Street in Nashville. Erv Woolsey owns the bar and donated it for the evening. It was amazing to see the number of well-wishers who showed up that evening to celebrate his thirty-year career in music. As I stated in my remarks that evening, "if the measure of a man is by the number of his friends, then David Haley was a very rich man." David passed away in May 2014 from a second massive stroke ten months following that retirement party.

At MCA, I hired several secondary promotion people, including J. W. Harper, Rick Hughes, Chuck Rhodes, Rosey Fitchpatrick, and Trudie Richardson Daniell. I used the secondary radio promotion team to call on *Gavin* or stations that reported to

Music Row magazine's chart, and to train young talent who desired to be regionals. This gave them experience they needed to develop relationships and hone their promotion skills before they competed in the high pressure *Billboard* and *R&R* reporting arena. Not only did it give us additional airplay exposure to create sales, it allowed me to nurture young people and move them up the ranks when job openings became available.

I believe that all airplay is good airplay. Since I grew up hearing music on small market radio stations, I know the important role those programmers play in developing an audience for an artist. I worked my first seven years at MCA without a national promotion director, even though all of the other country labels had one. Each year, I forfeited the director position so the marketing department could hire a sales or marketing rep.

I continued to build my promotion team, and made it the team to beat. No one could figure out what we were planning or doing next, or how we continued to break talent year after year. Every plan was customized to fit a particular artist and a particular song. And, it was all based on how the song made me feel while also playing off the strengths of the artist. We achieved successes that the industry thought impossible, set many new records, and exceeded our goals time and time again. In 1985, we celebrated fourteen number one singles and held that coveted spot for sixteen weeks.

With each success, I gained confidence. We fought hard as a team, and we were on our way.

Joe Deters, Rick Hughes, Lori Evans, me, George and Norma Strait, Roger Corkill, Rosey Fitchpatrick, Pat Surnegie, and David Haley

My buddy, Waylon Jennings

Ken Tucker, Conway Twitty, me, Pat Surnegie (MCA), and Dee Henry

Rick Hughes, Lyle Lovett, Patty Loveless, Tony Brown, David Haley

CHAPTER 10

Life at MCA

Soon after joining MCA, I received the news that my dad had been admitted to the Nashville VA Medical Center. He had been diagnosed with leukemia. While he had not been in my life for many of the important moments: graduation, baptism, wedding, or the birth of my son, it was me he called to help him get some things together to make him more comfortable in the hospital. I was the only person in Nashville that Dad knew, and I was okay with that. Daddy wanted a cassette player and some George Jones and Merle Haggard tapes, something he could warm soup or coffee in, and some magazines. I gathered them all and visited him while he was there.

Over the next year he was in and out of the hospital and during those times we never talked about anything serious. He never brought up the past, nor did I. One night in early 1985, he called me out of the blue. He said he wanted to tell me that he was proud of me, and that it wasn't Momma's fault that he left.

"She is a good woman and you are a lot like her," he said.

That was an important call for me. His words took me to a place where I could recover from all the childhood pain. It didn't completely plug the empty hole he left inside of me by his leaving, but it filled it a little, and I took the high road of forgiveness.

A few months later, the leukemia escalated and by March of the following year he had died. Maybe my dad knew his cancer was returning. Maybe a small voice told him to reach out while he still had time. Regardless, it was a call I will treasure for the rest of my life. I buried Daddy on March 1, 1986, the first day of Country Radio Seminar that year, then returned to Nashville to participate in the event. Life moved on, but I was sad.

I wish I could have had more time with my dad so I could better understand the choices he made. Because of his choices I had spent most of my life grieving for the father I had lost—once in life and once in death. There was nothing I could do for him now, so I returned to Nashville and focused on my work in hopes of dulling the pain. My closed chapter with my dad gave me very few answers.

By the time my dad passed away, Momma had recently remarried and my stepdad, Dolan Willoughby, had stepped into our lives. Dolan was a veteran of the Korean War and had never been married. He came into our lives at a time when it would be easier for most men to walk away. Momma was raising two young grandchildren and my sister continued her wild antics, often disrupting our lives with pain and worry. Dolan loved those grandchildren and raised them as his own. He made tremendous changes to Momma's life, building a second floor onto her house and helping her feed animals, raise a garden, and can vegetables each summer. We often traveled to see them, and they came to see us every few weeks, which kept the bond of family strong. One of my favorite memories is of a vacation we all took to Gulf Shores, Alabama and seeing my mom and stepdad run into the ocean hand-in-hand.

With my new income, Bennie and I had moved into a home in Brentwood, Tennessee, about fifteen miles south of Nashville. Michael had turned thirteen and was still struggling in school. Michael is highly intelligent, but began to skip classes he didn't care for. When we sat down with the counselors, we were told they had never seen a kid do what he was doing. He would skip English and come back for history, skip math and come back for R.O.T.C. It was a challenge to keep him interested in some of the classes. We tried private school, psychologists, and counselors, and along the way, Michael became hard for us to deal with as parents. He talked back and often cursed us when he didn't get his way. His teenage years were some of the hardest years I've faced. He said things to me that I would never want any other mother to hear. As successful as I was in business, I felt I was failing in all the important areas of my life. The more I tried, the more I could not find the solutions I needed at home.

After he was let go from his last radio job, Bennie began to dabble in free-lance commercial work, and felt he could double his income if he focused on it full-time. He also assured me that being there when Michael got home from school would give him the opportunity to watch our son closer, and perhaps prevent problems from occurring. After months of discussion and promises of how much better it would be, I reluctantly agreed. I became more of a sole support to the family while Bennie pursued his dreams, just as Bennie had supported me when I was struggling to find my career path. I was glad Bennie was home more for Michael, however, I continued to be torn between the pressures of my career and the struggles within my own family.

• • •

At work, we continued to grow and take on new ventures. One of the biggest events MCA ever did was the premiere of Roger Miller's Broadway musical *Big River*. Roger Miller was an iconic singer songwriter who changed the sound of country and pop music in the 1960s with songs such as "King of the Road," "Dang Me," and "England Swings." Miller's "Tall Tall Trees," was later recorded by Alan Jackson, while Brooks & Dunn covered his song "Husbands and Wives."

In addition to our mainstream country releases and soundtracks, we had the opportunity to promote the Broadway cast album of the production of *Big River*. The play would eventually win a Tony Award. The promotion of a Broadway musical was a first for a Nashville label, and one that we cherished for the prestige it afforded us. Every record label looks for anchor events to entertain programmers, further develop relationships, and establish the record company as a player. Such was the case for the excursion we undertook.

For months, my assistant Lori Evans and I worked and planned. We traveled to New York to scout out the hotel, and planned the strategy to walk hundreds of radio guests to the musical and back without losing them. We selected menus. We met with hotel sales personnel and theater managers. When all was ready, we flew in 160 program directors from across the country and coordinated flights and gates of arrival.

To streamline the arrivals, we posted staff in different airport terminals and ran limousines back and forth from airport to hotel. We also had a welcome suite prepared with light food and beverages for our guests. The first evening was open for our guests, to give them time to rest and enjoy the city. The next evening we were going to attend the opening night of *Big River* followed by dinner at one of my favorite restaurants Wally & Joseph's. It was one of the grandest evenings we ever planned, and it came off without a hitch. As a matter-of-fact, Rhubarb Jones, one of our Atlanta radio guests, stood up and toasted the group and said it was the most incredible day of his life.

Back at our hotel suite after dinner it was time for more drinks and conversation as the night wore on into morning. And then it happened. In the early morning hours of the next day, Tony Brown honored us with the appearance of the baby buffalo. Many of us had heard about the buffalo, but few had ever witnessed its appearance. I can't remember everyone who was still in the suite, but I do recall Lon Helton (chart editor for *R&R*), Coyote Calhoun from WAMZ in Louisville, some of my staff, and a few others who were still milling about and telling stories.

At some urging, Tony decided to indeed let us see his baby buffalo. He told us to stay in the room while he went out into the hallway. He told us that when he knocked on the door, we should open it and stand aside. So we waited. In a few minutes, we heard the knock. As the door opened wide, in charged Tony Brown. He was down on his knees and elbows with his hands and finger extended upward to create little horns on his head. We witnessed the baby buffalo as he stampeded into the room. Ah, the music business.

In September of 1986, exactly ten years to the month that I had started in the music business, I found myself on a plane headed to a Palm Springs sales distribution convention for MCA. Two weeks earlier, I had just been promoted to the position of vice president of national promotion—a position no other woman before me had ever held. I was the first, the exception to the rule. I had made it in a circle where no woman in country music had ever been accepted and where none had survived who had attempted. For a moment, I closed my eyes and recalled the years that had passed. Ten years before, I had started my first industry job as a receptionist with Monument Records. Ten years before I was told I could never become even a department manager at any music industry company. I sighed feeling proud that I had proven them all wrong. I had proven that hard work, honesty, and strong leadership could pay off—despite gender.

In 1988, I was nominated for an award at that year's *Gavin* convention. The Country Radio Seminar fell at the same time, so I was unable to attend *Gavin's* event. Larry Hughes was in Nashville attending the Country Radio Seminar. Since Larry lived in Los Angeles, he agreed to leave the Nashville convention early to fly out to attend the *Gavin* event for the label. Their convention was held in San Francisco, California each year, and this year he stopped off there before heading home.

The Saturday evening of the awards dinner I received a call from Larry, who said I had won the *Gavin* Country Vice President of Promotion of the Year award. I was both honored and shocked. The award was such a great honor, because it was voted on by radio and my industry peers. And it was a shock because I was recognized by the entire entertainment industry! I was honored with that same award two additional times, once in 1992 and again in 1994, just as I began my position at Decca Records.

• • •

Late in 1989, Tony Brown handed me a song to listen to and asked my opinion. When I was alone, I put the cassette into the tape player in my office and listened to one of the most magnificent voices I had ever heard. I felt a warmth run over me as I listened to the voice and begged Tony Brown to tell me he was signing the artist to MCA. The voice belonged to Mark Chesnutt, and the song was "Too Cold at Home."

MCA did sign Mark and that was to be his very first single. During this period of time, radio programmers were very passionate about new music. Within days of receiving new music, programmers listened and gave feedback. A few years later, the industry would begin its "dog and pony show" to radio, marching artists into radio stations to sing in their conference rooms. While MCA did host a few select artist showcases, most of our music was launched based on our own marketing creativity, a special song; and a dynamic, unique voice. This was also a time when programmers could still make choices about what they played in their individual markets.

Today, those choices are often made for them at a corporate level, despite what the local radio programmer may want to do.

That is often why you hear the same songs every time you listen to the radio. The result is that there are fewer stations willing to take a risk on new music, unless that music is from a major label.

In early 1990 I sat in my South Street office in the days when I still used my Selectric II typewriter, and personally typed two hundred fifty notes to radio programmers. Somewhere, filed away, I still have one of those notes. But I can still recall most of it from memory. I asked my radio friends to sit down in a quiet place and put Mark's cassette into a player and turn it up loud enough to listen. I told them that for me it had all the markings of a number one record: a special song and a special voice. I asked for three minutes of their time. I also asked them to call me and let me know what they thought.

One of the calls I received was from Lon Helton who at the time was the chart editor for *R&R*. He asked why I would step out, put my name on the line, and state that Mark's song was "a number one record." I told him that by everything I used to measure a number one hit, I felt it should be just that. Even if it didn't accomplish my goal, it would always be a should have been number one to me.

The song did go on to be a number one on one of the smaller charts, but we sat at number two for three consecutive weeks as Garth Brooks's "Friends in Low Places" held the number one position on *Billboard* and *R&R*. Timing is everything. Regardless, it was the song that launched a multitude of number one singles from Mark Chesnutt and led the way to his multi-platinum success.

Due to several explosive years in country music around the time we first released his music, Mark Chesnutt never received the industry awards and accolades that he truly deserved. In listening to the first three albums of his that MCA released, you will have listened to some of the best country music Nashville ever made.

But Mark's wasn't the only amazing voice I heard while at MCA. As Tony Brown often did, he asked me to attend a showcase for a young female artist he was interested in. He wanted Bruce Hinton and me to give him an opinion of the artist before a final decision was made. The artist was performing at a writers' night at a small club called Douglas Corner with hit songwriter Pat Alger, and was going to have a step out part during his show where she'd sing two or three songs.

That night I was enjoying Pat's songs, but I was also a bit antsy to see the young female singer who was handling Pat's background vocals. Tall and blonde, she carried a presence just standing in the shadows as a harmony singer. Finally, Pat introduced Trisha Yearwood and informed the crowd that she was going to perform a few songs.

I listened as one of the sweetest voices I have ever heard began to flow out of the microphone. By the end of her set, I was out of my seat and standing in the rear bar area talking to Tony Brown. In response to his "what do you think?" I said, "I'd sign her on a napkin tonight. She is a country Linda Ronstadt." Later, I saw that exact description of Trisha from several reviewers. Bruce Hinton was also over the top about her, so it was destiny that brought her to us—and the rest is history.

Garth Fundis was producing Trisha. Being the great song man that he is, he often held onto songs for years, hoping to find the right marriage of song and artist. Garth has produced many legendary artists, including Alabama, Don Williams, Sugarland, and Keith Whitley. He was also the director of operations for the record label Almo Sounds in the 1990s. When he produced a Don Williams project some years before, he had been pitched a song called "He's in Love With the Girl." He liked the song but didn't feel it was a fit for Don, so it got tucked away in a drawer. When he began working with Trisha, he pulled out the song and called the writer to ask if the lyric could be changed to "She's in Love With the Boy" to which the answer was, "absolutely."

Often, I stole ideas from our pop department, and they had recently sent out a combo package that included a video and disc of music. I decided that for Trisha, we should send out a box set of the single and video to all of our radio programmers. We never took Trisha on a single radio tour. In 1991 "She's in Love With the Boy" became the first of eight number one career singles for her. And, her first album netted an additional three top tens. Trisha Yearwood became a country superstar in the years that followed, and won three Grammys, three CMA awards, two ACM awards, and a Pollstar Industry Award for touring and selling over 12.5 million albums. She has also authored several cookbooks and hosts her own cooking show.

About the time that first Trisha Yearwood single was topping the charts, she came to see me in my office. We spoke about some personal issues she was experiencing, and about where she hoped her career was headed. That day she also told me she was divorcing her first husband. As so often happens, the young sweethearts had grown apart and it was time for each to go their separate way.

Trisha then asked me a question that caused me to begin planning *my* next career goal. She said she needed a new manager and wished it could be me. She said she knew she needed me there at MCA as her vice president of promotion, but wished I could leave to be her manager. She had met several times with Ken Kragen. Ken had managed Kenny Rogers and Lionel Richie for many years. I told her that he would open doors for her that most could never go through. She seemed happy that I respected Ken and felt it a good move for her to make. And it was a good move. Less than six months later Trisha was singing at the White House as part of their annual Christmas Gala. This was quite an accomplishment for a young Georgia singer who was celebrating the success of her first number one single.

At the time though, Trisha was in the infancy of her career and no one could project the success she would or would not have. I was at a major label living a dream come true and not financially stable enough to step out on my own as a manager. There were times when I wondered if I made the right decision. While I continued in my position at MCA, it was Trisha who taught me to dream beyond that job. It was that very day that I began to dream of running a label or starting my own management company. Little did I know then, but I would be able to do both.

In the meantime, Marty Stuart was an artist who had recorded for Columbia Records. After moderate success, Tony Brown decided to sign him to MCA. He believed he could cut a commercial record on Marty.

At the time, there were several independent record promotion companies used by labels to supplement the efforts of their in-house staff. I used Skip Stevens and Debbie Gibson Palmer quite a bit. Skip lived in Nashville while Debbie operated from Los Angeles. Occasionally, I used Sam Cerami. While it was our job to get records played, I liked to compare what the indie promoters were being told to what our staff was being told about our releases. About the time we were getting ready to release Marty Stuart's "Hillbilly Rock" single, I received a call from a young man who was doing independent promotion. His name was Scott Borchetta. Scott was the son of Mike Borchetta, who at one time was an executive at Curb Records here in Nashville. I consider Mike a friend, but he doesn't always handle situations the way I would.

Before former California Lieutenant Governor Mike Curb opened his office in Nashville, he found talented country singers and signed them to other labels, while still running his own Curb Records imprint. He had Hank Williams Jr. signed to Warner/Curb, The Judds to RCA/Curb, The Bellamy Brothers and Lyle Lovett to MCA/Curb, etcetera.

Mike Borchetta was an independent record promoter who was hired as vice president of promotion for Curb Records when they finally launched their fully staffed Nashville operation. Back then, when promotion people at other labels or independent promoters saw a record was without a bullet (which indicated a loss of momentum), or heard that a station had dropped a song from their playlist, they would tell the next station they spoke to "I heard that Glen Campbell record is over." This was an effort to create space to get their own record added at that station. Radio promotion is a very cut throat business, and we spent a lot of our time putting out the fires that other promoters started.

Such were my calls to Mike Borchetta, correcting him on the information he was spreading. I often called Mike to tell him our song was not over, and to stop telling radio that it was before he checked with me.

So, I was a bit skeptical of Scott, thinking he might be like his dad. A lot of independent promotion people regularly called me to ask to be hired on a song "because they needed the work." That did not bode well with me. As a matter of fact, in my book it worked against them. When Scott called, he said he had been in the studio the night before and heard "Hillbilly Rock." He loved it. He wanted to be part of the project so much that he offered to work it for free.

That got my attention. Not the free part, but the passion part. He got it. He loved the song. He wanted to be part of its success. I told him that he did not have to work it for free, but I would make him part of the team and hired him to work the single independently. Over the next few weeks I spoke to Scott daily. I watched him work. When one of the regionals got a song added that Scott thought wasn't close, he was the first to commend the regional for the effort. When he called in an add that he had secured, he was always excited about his news. I could see that he had developed relationships with radio, and I saw a fire in Scott that is vital to being successful in a national promotion job.

A promoter has to be able to see the big picture. He (or she) also has to be able to give credit where credit is due or the team will abandon him. Acknowledge true effort and a promoter will work harder for you, and often for less money, than the competition is willing to pay.

When it came time to hire my national director, I told Bruce Hinton that I wanted to hire Scott. I never interviewed another person. I remember calling Scott and inviting him to breakfast so we could talk. I offered him the job and I am still thrilled that he joined me in the next chapter of MCA's history-making success.

• • •

By early 1990, I realized that I was nearing the end of trying to make my marriage work. Bennie and I were like so many other couples who had grown apart over time. I was tired of being the father, mother, wife, sister, and bread winner. I was tired of traveling to conventions alone when my peer's spouses were traveling with them. I begged Bennie to go to counseling, only to be told time after time that there was nothing to talk about.

My brother Shelby had gone through a divorce about six months before and it was a real kick in the teeth for me. Shelby and I had both married the same year. While I was pondering all of this a friend told me that Bennie didn't think I would ever leave him. If I wanted Bennie to agree to work on our marriage, I knew I would have to present a real threat to the relationship if he was to take me seriously.

About this same time, Michael turned eighteen and married a young girl he'd known for about a year. He and his wife were both working full time and living with us, but was now at the age where he wanted his own life and he seemed to be moving in a direction to achieve that. While most of our family vacations had been driving trips to the Gulf of Mexico somewhere along the Alabama or Florida coast, Bennie and I had taken Michael to Mexico when he was ten. Bennie also flew with me to Miami once for a MCA convention.

Beyond that, it was difficult to get Bennie to enjoy what my salary could afford for us. He was always nervous about flying, but even so, I thought that a trip up the California coast was exactly what we needed. I also thought that taking my newly divorced brother along would entice Bennie to go, as he loved my brother as if he was his own. We could go to Universal and Hanna Barbara Studios in Los Angeles, and then drive up the coast highway to San Francisco. After all, this played into the cartoon and voice-over world that Bennie loved so well. To my surprise and delight, Bennie agreed. Tickets were purchased and hotels booked. I shopped and packed, and we headed to the Nashville airport in May of 1990. After checking our luggage, Shelby, Bennie, and I sat in the airport lounge waiting to board the plane.

Bennie seemed nervous and Shelby kidded him saying, “You need a drink.”

Bennie doesn’t drink much at all and laughed before he said, “I can’t go. There is no way I can get on that plane.”

With that, he stood up. Saying he was sorry, he told us to enjoy the trip and he would see us when we returned.

I was both angry and shattered, but, I was also determined that Shelby and I would have a good trip. We did enjoy those days together as siblings. I had VIP passes for Universal and we were moved to the front of the line. We ate great food and enjoyed the scenery as we told stories all the way up Highway One from Los Angles to San Francisco and across the Golden Gate Bridge. I took Shelby to all the places I had enjoyed on my business trips and shared with him the sites I always wanted to share with the man I loved. The trip took away some of the sadness Shelby was feeling after his divorce and gave us the chance to spend adult time as a brother and sister. The time passed quickly.

As Bennie’s luggage had already been loaded into the cargo hold of the plane, I schlepped his luggage in and out of the airport and in and out of hotels all the way up the coast of California.

Every time I saw that luggage, I became more and more hurt until I reached a decision that changed my family forever. My brother and I had married in the same year. Maybe we should also divorce in the same year.

On the plane home I compiled a letter to Bennie. I decided then and there that our life was not to continue as it had been. If we could not live and enjoy life together, then we could divorce and go our separate ways. Apparently, he wasn't getting what he needed from me, and I certainly wasn't getting what I needed from him. I wish I had known then that Bennie suffered from agoraphobia. I wish *he* had known. Maybe my decision would have been different.

A few days after we returned I had a business trip that called me out of town. Since Bennie and I could never sit down face to face to have a conversation without him leaving the room, I thought I would put my feelings in writing, then call him after I had landed. Once I got my bags and checked into the hotel, I called Bennie to get his reaction to my letter. I had hoped I would shake him up enough that he would finally tell me what he wanted and how we could recapture the love of our youth.

When I got him on the phone, I asked, "Did you read the letter I left you?"

"I did," he replied.

"Well, do you have anything to say?" I asked.

He was quiet for a moment then said, "There is no way I can survive a divorce. I will have to file bankruptcy. I can't believe you want to do this to me."

Whatever I might have intended to say vanished with those words. I expected something like, "I've loved you too long for us to do this. I can't live without you. We can go to counseling. We can fall back in love again." But I didn't hear any of those words. In silence, I felt the earth move under my feet. He didn't care if I left. He only cared that it would be a financial burden to him. In the end I did everything in my power to make sure my leaving was not a financial burden.

After getting our house appraised, I pulled all of his credit card debt into a second mortgage, which was about 50 percent of the equity. I bought new linens and pots and pans, and split up the furniture so he had whatever he needed. Even though my letter to him was in May, I did not file for divorce until October. We did not fight or argue that summer and were cordial to each other. He never asked to reconcile and I have always wondered what would have happened if he had.

December of nineteen ninety was when my divorce was final––after twenty-five years of being together. When two people live together that long they change, and if not careful, they can grow apart. When I told Michael about my decision to divorce, he understood. After all, he had been the strongest witness to our family life. Michael loved his dad, but they did not share a love of the same things. Michael was motorcycles, fishing, and outdoors. Bennie was cameras and technology. I am happy to report that they are now closer as adults than they were when we were all together. I am also glad that Bennie was there for Michael in some pretty dark times of his adult life following two difficult marriages and divorces.

New Years Eve of 1990, I was alone for the first time in my adult life and I found that I enjoyed making my own plans and decisions. I was excited by the opportunities that were ahead of me to grow as an individual and experience life as a single woman. My friend Bonnie Garner, who also managed Marty Stuart as well as The Highwaymen, called me right before the holidays and said that Marty wanted me to cover New Years' weekend with him. He had a couple of shows in Arkansas and thought it would be good for me to get out and not be alone. I appreciated his friendship, and for caring enough to ask me to go out with his guys.

Because bus drivers are paid a day rate, artists' buses roll out of town at midnight to save an extra day's pay. I am usually in bed by ten o'clock so it was a challenge for me to just stay awake long enough to get to the bus. We arrived at 100 Oaks Shopping Center where the musicians all left their cars in the parking lot. As we headed out of Nashville at midnight on December 30th, the roads were icy and there was much more snow and ice to come between our destination and us. All night I felt the bus slide back and forth as we hit patches of ice. At one point I got up from my bunk, and went up front to sit with the driver for a while as he navigated between the icy spots on the road.

Entering the New Year as a single woman was a new experience. All my friends encouraged me to date, to get out and have some fun. After all, I had never experienced that and the concept appealed to me. However, I was quite content in my new-found freedom and wasn't concerned with finding Mr. Right anytime soon. I had my career and a lifetime of marriage. If I didn't ever find Mr. Right, I knew I would be just fine. No marriage is better than a bad marriage.

My friends told me I would have to find a strong man, one who was confident in who he was, or he would be overwhelmed by my success. I knew that was true. After all, being married to a high-profile woman is not easy for most men. After a few dates, I figured out that the dating scene wasn't very pleasant. I don't play games and am instead a direct and honest person. After a few missteps in the dating arena, I swore off the whole man thing.

My assistant, Lori Evans, had been telling me about a guy I should go out with. She had attempted to go out with him a few times, but finally figured out that they were not a good fit. He worked in Christian music, owned a publishing company called Copperfield Music, and was a nice guy. She described him as a tall man with gray hair and a gray beard. I instantly thought *not my type*. I never followed up on her suggestion to call him, forgot about the conversation, and went on with my day-to-day routine.

* * *

One Saturday morning I was cleaning my house in Brentwood when I heard the news that a plane carrying members of Reba McEntire's band and crew had crashed on the side of Otay Mountain near San Diego, California. It was March 16, 1991. Chills ran up and down my spine as the television announcer assured viewers that Reba and her husband and manager Narvel Blackstock had not been on the plane when it departed. But, the crash had taken the lives of eight members of her band. Chris Austin, Kirk Cappello, Joey Cigainero, Paula Kay Evans, Jim Hammon, Terry Jackson, Anthony Saputo and Michael Thomas, along with pilot Donald Holmes and co-pilot Chris Hollinger, were all killed when the charter jet they were flying to the band's next gig crashed.

I can't imagine how it would feel to lose that many people in one accident. People you worked and played with and traveled with for years. Reba suffered the anguish of that loss and stated recently that she still grieves for each and every one of them. She said the one lesson it taught her is to cherish every day. That is a lesson we can all learn, because we never know what each day will bring. It could be the loss of a loved one through a sudden illness, a car crash, or a plane wreck that steals someone near and dear away.

In October 1991, we released Reba's album *For My Broken Heart*. A lot of reviewers said it had a dark nature, but it was Reba's way of dealing with the loss of those she loved. I think it was one of her best albums ever and should have been awarded Album of the Year.

With my mentor, Jimmy Bowen

With Marty Stuart and Zach Horowitz (CEO, MCA)

David Haley, Lionel Cartwright, Mark Collie, Steve Wariner, and Don Light

CHAPTER 11

Personal Changes

It is strange how fate can change our destinies without our even knowing it. In July of 1991 I was invited to go out after work with a group from MCA. The group often went out in the evenings and I had never met them for one of their after-hours events. The marketing department, led by Walt Wilson, was all in tow that night along with John Lytle from our administration department, Tony Brown, Lori Evans, and several others.

Walt was responsible for the sales and marketing plans for each of our releases. He loved to party and created an atmosphere where his workers excelled in creativity. He also loved to get them out together at night so everyone could let their hair down. Often after a night of such revelry, they ended up back at the MCA office to continue into the wee hours of the night.

John Lytle was a bright young man from Texas who had entered MCA as an intern, and who worked his way into our administration department. John came to town with a plan to learn all he could about label operations before becoming an artist manager, just as Erv Woolsey had done with George Strait several years before. I admired the fact that John had crafted a plan for his life and was fulfilling it step by step.

That night, we met on the patio of Sunset Grill, an upscale industry hangout and one of the few places in Nashville that featured outdoor dining in 1991. An hour or so into our visit, Lori went inside to the bathroom along with Jennifer Stuart, Marty Stuart's sister. Both came out giggling and telling me that my Mr. Right was inside. I continued to tell them I that I had no interest in Mr. Right.

More time passed, then they went back inside to the bathroom again, and when they returned they did so with a very tall man in tow. This was the man they wanted me to meet. And yes, he was tall with gray hair and a gray beard. He was attractive, but I wasn't in the mood for either attractive or unattractive guys at that moment. As he approached me to say hello, I extended my hand.

He put his arms around me, pulled me up to him and kissed me on the mouth.

"I thought you said he wasn't like this," meaning a cad, I said to Lori.

"I've never seen him act that way," she replied.

I looked up at Ken Biddy. "Well, aren't you something?"

He came right back with, "And don't you forget it."

We exchanged business cards, me with the intent of him giving me a call in a few days.

I had been reading a book about dating and one of the tips it mentioned was about men asking you out. It suggested that lunch is often better than dinner, because you have to return to work and often the awkwardness of the goodbye at the end of an evening can be avoided. I thought this was a good idea, since I had been cornered a few times after a dinner. I promised myself to have a lunch date the next time I went out with anyone I did not know well. I was in my office on the phone when Pat Payne came in with a note that read KEN BIDDY IS ON THE PHONE. I told her to tell him that I would call him back.

When I finished my phone call, I dialed his number and he immediately came on the line. Little did I know, but Ken thought I was avoiding him when I didn't take his call. He had pulled my business card out to look at it and realized I was a vice president at MCA. When he placed the call, he felt I would not take it, nor would I return it. Well, here I was returning the call within minutes of him leaving a message. He seemed both impressed and delighted.

Ken invited me to lunch the next day. Before I called, I was tensely anticipating whether he would ask me out for lunch or dinner and then there it was: lunch. I graciously accepted his invitation, and he suggested he pick me up at eleven-thirty the next day.

Ken showed up at my office as scheduled. He was dressed in slacks and a long sleeved shirt with suspenders, and I thought he was quite handsome. And, I was surprised by how much I had looked forward to our lunch date. We returned to Sunset Grill and sat in a booth in the bar area where we would have more privacy. As we began to share our life stories, Ken told me about his two broken marriages, and what had led to their ends. He spoke to me about his children, and the heartbreak of losing custody of them. He deeply felt the loneliness that only a parent can feel when he cannot hold his children on a daily basis.

Ken said he used to stand over his daughter Dena's crib at night and cry, because he missed her so much when she was at her mother's. He spoke of his first marriage, and how for five years he had lived a separate life only to reconcile one evening during which his wife became pregnant. Throughout the pregnancy, he believed, or wanted to believe, the child belonged to someone else. As I listened to his pain, I was drawn into the soul of man I was listening to. Ken was honest and vulnerable, and shared details usually too intimate and personal for casual conversation. He trusted me enough to recall and share his years of pain and loss. At the conclusion of his story, he told about finally holding the baby and looking into Daniel's eyes. He said at that moment he knew Daniel was his son. Deep down, Ken had known it all along.

Of course, by this time I could not contain the tears that filled my eyes. They began to run down my cheek as I listened, then I wiped them from my face. Ken says he knew at that moment that I was the woman he would marry. He had been single for eight years and had sworn off marriage, running anytime a woman got too attached or too close. Now, he was looking at me and sensing feelings that I did not share—yet.

During our lunch, Ken commented on my hands, saying they and my nails were beautiful. He asked if I got manicures to which I replied, "I've never had one." I told him I did them myself and really needed to get a manicure kit sometime, but always forget to pick one up when I was out shopping. He listened and smiled, and soon it was time to return to work. Before we parted, though, we made a date for Saturday evening. I was leaving town to attend the Mid-West Conclave in Minneapolis, but was coming back Saturday morning. The Conclave is a multi-format radio convention that takes place each July, and I was a guest speaker on one of the country panels that year. Ken was attending an early wedding that Saturday, but said he would pick me up about eight P.M.

About an hour after I returned to work, I was at my desk when Pat Payne walked in and said that Ken Biddy was there to see me. A little shocked, I got up and walked out to meet him in the atrium, where he proceeded to give me a manicure kit. I smiled and thanked him, but I was taken back at such a gift from someone I barely knew. Little was I to know that Ken's generosity would continue in the years ahead as he always provided me with cards, small gifts, or flowers when I least expected it. After my thank you he was gone. Now I was *really* looking forward to Saturday evening.

I had barely finished speaking on my panel when I became ill. I was so sick that I decided to return home as soon as possible and was home Friday morning instead of Saturday. A good night's rest, and I was much better by Saturday and our appointed date. I was relieved, as I had not wanted to cancel.

When Ken arrived at my home in Brentwood that Saturday evening, I walked outside and down the front walk to meet him. That was a first, he said. He had never had a woman walk outside to meet him before. Instead, he usually met his dates at their door. As I wasn't versed in the ways of dating, and didn't really care what other women did on dates, I followed my own heart and felt quite comfortable in welcoming him the way I did. Then I invited Ken inside to meet my son Michael, who was now eighteen and already divorced.

Michael wasn't too happy about me dating, so he grunted a few words and went back to his video game. While Michael accepted the divorce, it was hard for him to see me dating other men. He had met a couple of them and was protective of me because he didn't want to see me get hurt. I told him goodbye and Ken and I left my house for our first dinner date.

Ken opened the car door for me and we backed out of the driveway. Ken had chosen Sperry's Restaurant in Belle Meade. I loved Sperry's, and was delighted at the choice. The restaurant has an old world feel, and is a romantic place for a quiet dinner. This would be an unrushed opportunity to get to know one another. I was certainly not in any hurry to tie myself to one man, but I thoroughly enjoyed the attention I was receiving. After all, I had been with one man for twenty five years, well over half my life.

We had a beautiful evening together comparing notes on who we both knew in the music business. Ken told me that he had known Lori Evans for a long time. He said that he and Lori were actually supposed to have gone out one evening for a date. She had called the night Reba's plane had crashed and said she couldn't make it because she needed to stay close in case she was needed. Ken said they both realized they weren't a good fit for each other and never rescheduled the ill-fated evening.

During our date, we spoke of faith, shared more of life's heartbreaks and pleasures, and by end of evening Ken had totally enchanted me. Not wanting the evening to end, he said he did not want to be forward, but would like to invite me back to his condo to listen to some music if I felt comfortable doing that. By now I trusted Ken and told him I would enjoy that very much. When we arrived, he pulled out some of his favorite CDs and played songs from Michael Bolton and Roseanne Cash. We danced and talked some more and I ended up spending the evening with him.

The next day, Ken asked me to go shopping with him for an antique table that he wanted for the upstairs landing of his townhouse. The next morning while we were drinking coffee, Lori called to make sure we were okay. It was so out of character for me not to check in at home that Michael had called her when I had not returned after our date. He thought I might be out with an axe murderer and wanted to see if she knew Ken. After assuring her all was well, I called home and assured my son that I was indeed well and would be back later that afternoon.

Ken and I spent most of the day looking in shops. Then we stopped at McDonalds for a quick burger before we headed home. I had barely settled in that evening when Ken called to invite me back to his house. Because the next day was a work day, he suggested I bring clothes and change for work the next morning from his home. It sounded like a good plan and it was one that was repeated several times until Ken made room in his closet and asked me to move in. Michael had recently joined the National Guard and was in Ft. Knox, Kentucky in basic training, so the timing seemed right to make a change in my life.

During those first weeks, often Ken went to my house to feed Iggy, Michael's iguana. He then suggested we bring Scooter to the townhouse with me. Scooter was my eight-year-old Yorkie, whom I adored. The fact that Scooter took to Ken so quickly probably pushed me over the edge to finally admit how much I loved Ken. I didn't want to love him, because it felt as if it was way too soon for me to care, to lock myself down to one person. On the other hand,

I didn't want to walk away from a good man just because the timing wasn't right.

In September, Ken traveled with me to Canada for the Canadian Country Music Awards. Later that month we traveled to Puerto Vallarta, Mexico on vacation. Soon the CMA Awards, which are held in Nashville, were upon us. MCA always hosted a huge party for our artists, staff, industry celebs, and out-of-town guests. That particular year, the party was held in the ballroom of the Lowes Vanderbilt Hotel on West End Avenue. As was the occasion on event nights like CMA, I had a hotel room in town and planned to dress there after work. It was also my birthday, October 2, 1991 so the party would be additionally festive. Ken and I had been dating for three months.

When we arrived at the hotel, Ken asked me to stand outside while he got things ready. He was back at the door in a flash. He then opened the door for me to view his handy work. Inside the room, Michael Bolton was playing on the stereo, and Ken had filled the room with dozens and dozens of white roses. Along one end of the room was a banner wishing me a Happy Birthday. I couldn't believe he had gone to all that trouble to surprise me, and he assured me the surprises were not over.

We dressed and readied ourselves to go downstairs to meet my staff for our annual photos. I was wearing a red and black beaded dress and Ken a beautiful black tuxedo. He looked very regal and sophisticated. As we were about to leave, Ken said he had one more surprise and asked me to sit down in a chair. Then he quickly dropped to one knee and opened the small ring box in his hand and asked me to marry him. I stared at the beautiful princess cut diamond ring that was surrounded by diamond baguettes. With tears in my eyes, I promised him forever at that very moment. We were married four short months later on February 1, 1992.

Ken is a man who is strong willed and strongly opinionated. While that can often cause conflict in our relationship, he is also as stalwart as an oak tree and can always be relied upon. Despite his strength, Ken has a soft heart and is the most generous person I have ever known, and he has provided me more than my heart could ever hope for or need.

During that summer and fall, we visited the Woodstock, Georgia area to meet Ken's huge family. I have never seen so many brothers and wives and children, all with names I hoped to remember. The first time I met his parents, they both came out onto the porch to greet us as we pulled in the driveway. I liked them immediately, and they appeared to feel the same way about me. Ken said he had never seen them act that way with anyone he had brought for a visit. I have a feeling he told them he was very serious about this one!

Ken's oldest daughter, Dena, was working and dating her now husband, Jeff Bryant, when we first met. Ken's oldest son, Daniel, and his daughter Amanda were still in high school, so I got to see both of them graduate over the next few years.

After our engagement in October we began to look for a new home to start our lives together. I put my Brentwood home up for sale and he listed his townhouse. We found a new two-story house on an acre lot in Brentwood and wrote a contract. It was a dream come true when both of our homes sold in time for us to move in by mid-December of 1991. Michael graduated from basic training and moved in with his dad for a few months.

Ken and I moved into our new home on December 12, and by December 22 everything was unpacked and put away. As was my usual custom, my Kentucky family drove down for an early Christmas dinner. We were so excited to share our new home with my family.

As we were returning from our Georgia Christmas trip in December 1991, we talked about when to get married. While it was short notice, we decided to marry on February 1, 1992 less than thirty-five days away. I thought nothing of it. I am one of those type A personalities so I figured I could pull it off. Ken wanted a church wedding, and since I had not had it the first time around I thought it was an excellent idea. Silly me. I had no idea how much planning it takes to pull off a wedding, or how expensive it can be.

We decided to marry at Brentwood Baptist Church. Mike Glenn had been the pastor there for about seven months and we did pre-marital counseling with him. That felt strange to me but I also welcomed the foundation it provided us. Using one example, Mike looked to me and said, "Ken can talk about his mother and be aggravated at her and even use strong words to describe her, but remember, blood is thicker than water. If you want to be happy together, don't ever join in and say something bad about his mother. While *he* can get away with it, he will never tolerate you saying disparaging things about her. The same will be true of your own mother or family member. We all think we are open minded enough to hear the truth, until it is turned on someone we love." I thought that piece of wisdom to be one every married couple should understand.

I did not want to spend a lot of money on a dress I would only wear one time, so I found a company in Nashville that did rentals of wedding and bridesmaid dresses, and formal gowns. That made sense to me. With invitations printed and a wedding dress on hold for the big day, we were well on our way to having the big stuff checked off our list.

As we began to plan our reception, though, things became a bit harder. Even though we are both in the music business and around alcoholic beverages all the time, Ken's father and mother, who were in their eighties, insisted on not having alcohol around them. They often made statements when we took them out to eat such as, "You know they sell spirits here." To which Ken would say, "Those spirits are not going to jump out and bite you, Mother."

Out of respect for them, we opted to have a reception at the church where no spirits would be served. Instead, we had cake and punch. We always said we would have an industry reception later, but somehow that idea drifted away. We did have lots of nice parties at our Brentwood home for friends and business associates, so every celebration like that was one I enjoyed more than I would have a big reception.

With out-of-town parents, uncles, and aunts squared away at our Brentwood home, Ken and I spent our wedding night at a Sheraton Hotel in Brentwood. In a week, we had the *Gavin* Convention in San Francisco so we planned to go out a few days early for our honeymoon. It was a way of combining a little work and pleasure in the same trip. I finally got to share some of the wonderful experiences of that city with the man I loved. We walked along the wharf, crossed the Golden Gate Bridge, saw the redwoods, and toured the wine country. Ken drove me down the coast highway for an afternoon before settling in to the radio convention for the weekend. I always thought we'd make it back to San Francisco, but sadly, so far, we never have.

• • •

After the wedding I settled back into life at MCA. We broke a lot of talent in the years I was at the helm of MCA's promotion department: Mark Chesnutt, Trisha Yearwood, Steve Earle, Patty Loveless, Lyle Lovett, Marty Stuart, Mark Collie, Nancy Griffith, The Mavericks, David Lee Murphy, Tracy Byrd, and Wynonna all saw the launch of their careers from within those walls.

In addition to the signing of new talent, we also signed legendary artists such as Conway Twitty, Loretta Lynn, Waylon Jennings, and George Jones. In 1991, we discussed signing George Jones and the challenges we would face in trying to release singles to radio. While George had celebrated tremendous radio success in his career, radio was no longer interested in playing legend artists. We had faced that with Loretta, Waylon, and to a lesser degree, Conway. Radio was much more interested in new and developing talent. They wanted to be part of the launch of tomorrow's stars, not yesterday's. But George wasn't ready to hang it up musically. He continued to tour extensively and he wanted the support of country radio.

While we wrestled with the challenges we would face, the opportunity to work with The Possum and release new music won out. By this point, George had married Nancy Sepulveda, and Nancy was handling George's management and business affairs. She was a brilliant business-person who had a strong sense of what worked for George. She knew when to push him for something that was needed in the marketing plan, and when to back off.

We decided to release the single, "I Don't Need Your Rockin' Chair," as it epitomized what Jones was feeling in his career at that point. He was a viable artist who wasn't ready to sit on the porch. He continued to tour extensively and he wanted another opportunity to be atop the charts. While the song peaked at number thirty-four, it was an anthem that caused many other artists to rally to the side of Jones in support. The song was much bigger than the position it reached on the charts, and became a moving statement for the aging Jones.

Ken and I became close to Nancy and George during the few years we worked together. We saw him in concert in the US and at a show in Toronto, Canada. When they were building their beautiful home in Franklin, Nancy gave us the gate code to check on the property while they were touring. While George didn't always remember names, he knew the people who supported him. Nancy often talked to him about something I had said, or an idea I had, to support the single. He'd then say to her, "Isn't that the girl down at MCA that loves me so much?" Love and respect him I did. The world will sadly miss this country music statesman. No one will ever fill his shoes.

Speaking of sadly missed, during my years at MCA, I had the honor to work with Conway Twitty. Bowen had recorded with him at Warner Brothers Records and when Bowen moved to MCA, Conway followed. We released several albums with Conway and took two singles to number one: "Julia" in 1987, and "I Couldn't See You Leavin' in 1991. My favorite single with Conway was "That's My Job." The first time I heard it on my advance studio cassette, I cried my eyes out. I thought it was the most beautiful song I had heard in years, and knew it was destined to be a single.

I remember standing outside the conference room after a staff meeting when Bowen asked me what I felt we should release from that particular Conway album. He asked me about several up tempo songs and I told him "That's My Job" was the song I wanted to lead with. He smiled and said if I believed in it that much to call Conway to let him know. Conway was delighted with my choice, and said it was his favorite too. While the song peaked at number six on the *Billboard* chart, to me it had a far greater impact on people than many songs that achieved number one. Even to this day I run across young singers who talk about the importance of that song in their lives.

Later, we were in the process of planning another release for Conway's final album for MCA, so I called Conway one Friday afternoon to discuss it with him. I had some ideas about setting up conference calls with radio programmers where they could ask him questions about the new project and have an inside scoop. Conway loved the idea and said he would come by my office the following Monday to discuss it. However, Friday afternoon was the last time I ever spoke to him.

On Saturday morning, my home phone rang about eight-thirty. It was Nancy Jones. She was calling to tell me the horrible news that Conway Twitty had died the night before in Springfield, Missouri on the way back from a show. Dee Henry, Conway's wife and manager, had called Nancy and asked her to let me know. It was then that I began the task of calling Bruce Hinton, Tony Brown, and others to brace them with the news before they heard it elsewhere. It was another sad moment in MCA history. It is hard to believe that more than twenty years have passed since Conway left this earth.

• • •

In March 1993, I was at the Opryland Hotel in promotion meetings when Bruce Hinton called to tell me he had received the staff payroll increases and wanted to meet with me to go over them. We scheduled a time and Bruce met me in the suite. After giving me the percentages and salary increases for the staff, he started to talk to me about an idea. By now, MCA was breaking an act every year and releasing a single every week. If we were to continue to grow, he wanted to launch a second imprint with a separate promotion staff. The new label would be called Decca Records.

Decca is an old name in music. The name had been shelved in 1972 when Owen Bradley was its general manager. The parent corporation decided to close the Decca imprints nationwide, but told Owen he could keep the name active for the Nashville division. The rest of the divisions would be changed to MCA. Owen told them he did not want a different name for the Nashville division. Despite the success he was having in Music City, it was difficult enough getting respect for his country artists without being the only division releasing product under the old Decca name.

Owen Bradley fought hard for Nashville's country division to be treated just like the company's other divisions. So, the artists who recorded for Decca at the time (Conway Twitty, Loretta Lynn, and Patsy Cline) were moved to the MCA imprint and the Decca label name was shelved. (Patsy Cline died in a plane crash in 1963, but the label continued to release catalog product on her.) The

Decca label name remained golden and had no tarnish or bad karma associated with it.

Bruce asked me to draft two business plans for the label. One would be fully staffed and the second would be with promotion, A&R, and publicity personnel, while sharing back-room services for the other departments that included marketing, sales, and creative services. Labels had tried launches both ways, but more recently sharing administrative and marketing responsibilities had proven more cost effective. He also asked me to give him a positioning statement for the roster, and a plan to develop those artists.

Bruce then went on to say that I could remain as senior vice president of promotion for the rest of my career. "As long as you continue to have chart success," he said, "you will have a secure position with MCA. Or, you could take a chance on a new venture." I was beyond thrilled when Bruce offered me the opportunity to be the general manager for the new label imprint. While Bruce's words echoed that this new venture would be a gamble, I thought back to Joe Galante's advice to me years earlier. As I had told Galante ten years before, I now reiterated the words to Bruce that the gamble would be on me. I welcomed the opportunity.

When Bruce left the room, my head was spinning with ideas. I was so excited I felt I could levitate at any minute. I was buzzing from one extreme to another, and could not wait for the convention to end so I could begin to draft a plan for the future.

Throughout the remainder of 1993, Bruce and I met often. We discussed artist rosters and flagship artists, and we talked about producers whose vision would complement the direction we shared for the label. Bruce had been a twenty-five-year long friend of Paul Worley and loved his production and his personality. He felt we would complement one another and reached out to him to investigate his interest. Paul was Bruce's first choice for the label A&R head. At the time, Paul was working for Sony Tree Publishing and successfully producing Gary Morris, Highway 101, The Nitty Gritty Dirt Band, Desert Rose Band, and Collin Raye. He was also a premiere guitarist in great demand on Nashville recording sessions. After several meetings, however, we became aware that Sony had other plans for Paul. He was named as one of the heads of Sony Records Nashville, along with Scott Simon and Allen Butler. Scott was a renowned Nashville attorney and Allen had been vice president of promotion during the successful launch of Arista Nashville. So, meetings took place with other producers.

At my suggestion, Tony and Bruce agreed to meet with Mark Wright. Both of them believed Mark Wright to be a great record producer, but they were unsure how he would fit into a corporate culture. Mark was known to be a party animal, and his character was colorful. We discussed moving either Mark Chesnutt or Trisha Yearwood over to Decca as its flagship artist, and eventually decided Mark Chesnutt would be the best fit since his traditional voice was a continuation of the strong country music legacy began earlier at Decca Records, when Owen Bradley had been at its helm.

Bruce agreed to meet with producer Mark Wright, and told me that he planned to invite Mark to dinner at his home to discuss the situation. He felt it best to meet with him privately as Bruce had questions he needed to ask that needed honest answers. If the answers sounded good, then we could all meet together. Whether it was true or not, I always believed that Bruce wanted to make sure Mark didn't have a problem working for a woman, although it may have been that he needed to know the animal could be chained if Mark came inside the label.

Bruce gave me total autonomy to develop the label from the very first step of designing the logo to its positioning statement. I decided on a royal blue and gold lettering that reflected the 1930s logo, but modernized the lettering to fit the style of the 1990s. While I met with the designers, I also made plans to hire staff, and I began to think about who would join me in writing this new chapter in history.

By the end of 1993, MCA had grossed 143 million dollars in sales from the Nashville office. In less than ten years, we had doubled the gross revenue of the division. We had grown and broken new talent that was now selling millions of albums annually with each of their releases. While George Strait, Reba McEntire, and Vince Gill had released singles prior to our regime's arrival, we developed them to multi-platinum superstar status. In 1993, each of these acts were selling six figures a week in CD sales, celebrating at least three number one singles per year, and winning every award that the Academy of Country Music and Country Music Association offered.

In my last year as senior vice president of promotion, we looked back on 1993 with spectacular chart success. We achieved fifteen number one singles from eight different artists that included George Strait, Vince Gill, Wynonna, a Vince Gill/Reba McEntire duet, Mark Chesnutt, Trisha Yearwood, and Reba McEntire. MCA had been named the number one country label for three consecutive years. Yes indeed, 1993 was a very good year. No other Nashville label could catch us, or even equal us, in chart or sales success. We were definitely the leader of the pack.

For most of 1992 and 1993, Bruce Hinton and Tony Brown met with developers who were building new office space on Music Row that would house our growing label. Offices were designed and measured and moved from one square on the plat to another. I would never move into my new second floor office at MCA. By the time the building was complete in December 1993 my office had been moved to the 1st floor, where Decca Records was to be housed.

As December 1993 came to a close, the baton was handed off to Scott Borchetta to lead the promotion department. After ten years of leading that team to its coveted number one position, I once again began a new chapter in my career.

This is the summer of 1991. Ken asked me to marry him about two months after this trip to California.

Ken Biddy and I with George Jones at an Atlanta concert.

Ken asked me to marry him at The Lowes Vanderbilt Hotel just before we headed out to the CMA Awards on October 2, 1991. Vince Gill congratulated us at the MCA party afterwards.

With George & Norma Strait, Bill Monroe, and Bruce Hinton

With Joe Deters, my beloved SE Regional

CHAPTER 12

Decca

During the Christmas holiday break, I prepared myself for my new venture at the helm of a label. It was a dream I had only begun to dream a short three years before when I sat down in my promotion office with Trisha Yearwood. The days seemed to creep by as I awaited the start of the New Year. Midnight took on a special meaning as 1993 slipped away into a closed chapter of MCA Records history. On January 2, 1994, I drove my dark green BMW into the parking space of the new MCA building at 60 Music Square East. It was my first day as the senior vice president and general manager of Decca Records. A TV news crew stood ready in the parking lot to chronicle the moment for the evening news: the first woman to head a record label in Nashville. Excitement and pride could not begin to express what I was feeling. I was almost giddy on adrenaline as I entered the building for my first day.

The first week I was in the job, I received a call from a long-time radio friend named Barry Mardit. Barry had been music and program director for WEEP in Pittsburgh, Pennsylvania when I was at RCA. He was the programmer who told me that he never had a promotion rep tell him they didn't like a record they were working. He was also the one who added that stinker of a song and gave me a chance to begin my promotion career. We had stayed friends for fifteen years and he had supported many, many great songs throughout the year.

That day, Barry said, "I am so proud of you. I don't know what your first single will be on Decca Records, nor do I know the date you will go for adds. Just know I will be holding a slot for that record the day you officially go for reports on the single. I want to be the first to add a Decca single." And he was. He added Dawn Sears "Runaway Train" a few months later. While we did not break Dawn to the level we hoped, we did have the most added single that week and the most added female song that year. Thank you, friends.

The first few months in the job never slowed down. Each day was absolutely crazy with so much to organize and complete. Lori

Evans moved with me to Decca, but was in charge of the publicity area of the label. I did not have a personal assistant yet, so I was answering my own calls, interviewing potential staff, and developing plans for the label. Mark Wright and I were both listening to new music submissions and attending showcases to look for that special voice that we knew would be part of our history.

Traditional country singer Dawn Sears had been signed to MCA. Because of their workload, MCA had not yet released a single on her. Since she fit the direction of the new Decca, Tony Brown, now president of MCA and head of A&R, asked that she be moved to our roster. He believed her to be a better fit for us, and MCA was back logged with releases. Mark and I both loved Dawn's voice and gladly agreed. Our first Decca recording session took place with Dawn Sears on February 7, 1994. The first single from Dawn was "Runaway Train," and released an album called *Nothing But Good* in August of that year.

Frank Liddell became our director of A&R. Mark Wright had known him at Blue Water Music Publishing and hired him to be our song guy on the inside. Frank had been a huge part of Blue Water's success, and obtained countless single cuts by major recording artists. As part of the A&R department, it was Frank's job to meet with songwriters and music publishers, and listen to new songs that could be recorded by our artists. Frank had an incredible ear for a hit, and a heart as big as Texas. Frank later became an incredible producer in his own right and ended up marrying the talented Lee Ann Womack.

A few months after we opened our doors, Mark asked me to come into his office and listen to a young man named Rhett Akins. Mark really liked his voice and wanted my opinion. Rhett was a songwriter for Sony/Tree, a huge music publishing company, and had been offered a contract with Sony Nashville. Mark said that while Rhett had a record contract in hand, he was "Just like a woman who's engaged. Until she has that wedding band on her finger, she's fair game."

I loved Rhett's voice, and I loved the way he crafted a song. We scheduled a meeting for January 31, 1994. When Mark set up his office, he wanted it to have a creative feel. He had a desk where he could work on paperwork and answer the phone, but the rest of the office was more laid back. He had an oriental rug on the floor, a coffee table complete with a large ceramic cowboy hat, a sofa, and a couple of soft chairs. There was also a bright red ceramic razor back pig in the corner because Mark was from Arkansas and proud of it. He also had one of those bright red razor back pig hats too, the kind with the big snout that hangs out over your face.

Rhett sat in Mark's office, pulled out his guitar, and played us his songs. On the spot, we offered him a home with Decca—if he wanted it. He was so excited about our enthusiasm. He understood that we got his music and what he was about as an artist. He told us that Sony Nashville had offered him a recording deal and had already sent him a contract. I laugh when I think about it but Mark didn't miss a beat.

"Have you signed it yet?" Mark asked.

Rhett said he had not, to which Mark said, "Good." Rhett laughed, and I was thrilled that Rhett rejected the deal Sony offered and agreed to sign to sign with us.

In that first get-to-know-you meeting, Rhett told us he had met with Narvel Blackstock (Reba's husband and manager) and tried to convince Narvel to accept him as a management client. Narvel told him that until he had a label deal, there was nothing to manage. That is not uncommon in Nashville. Many managers refuse to manage an act that does not have a deal. First, they don't want to take the time and energy to schedule label meetings and go through the process, only to be rejected. It is not a matter of how much a prospective manager might believe in an artist. The problem is finding a label that shares that belief.

Second, it takes years for the artist to begin making money, and it does not make business sense for a manager to commit to an artist unless there is a label deal. In recent years, with the success of artists from shows such as *American Idol* and *The Voice*, labels want to hit the fast forward button on artist development. Labels want to sign artists that have become household names and built fan bases by appearing on these national television shows week after week. Producers rush in and record a song that labels push to market the week after the show concludes, hoping to tap into sales while viewers are still aware of and supportive of the artist.

Radio is more receptive to these artists as well, since they have become household names during the competition. Prior to these reality shows, labels developed artists by teaching them how to handle media interviews, coached them on their live performance, and extensively showcased or radio toured with them for six months to a year before releasing a single. This is a very expensive and time-consuming process that does not always have a successful end result.

In the case of Rhett and Narvel, the marriage between artist and manager was perfect. After all, Narvel managed Reba on the MCA side and with Rhett on the sister label, there were a lot of synergies we could develop between the two artists and labels. Once Rhett had accepted the Decca offer, Narvel gladly accepted him as a management client.

On December 22, 1994, we shipped Rhett's first single "That Ain't My Truck" to radio. By early summer, we were still working the single when Ken and I flew to Hawaii for a much needed vacation. Vince Gill was doing a show on the island and Dawn Sears was singing background vocals. It seemed again to be the perfect time to combine work and pleasure. Lori Evans and her husband Carl Massaro also went. I told the staff to take care of things and call only if they had to.

There is a five-hour time difference between Nashville and Hawaii. We arrived on Saturday and by Tuesday my cell phone was ringing. We had several radio stations that wanted to drop Rhett's single. They felt they had been on the record too long and were ready to come off. I found myself calling stations, arguing, and begging them to give us more time. I remember sitting by the pool and running down cell batteries in an attempt to save the record. Other hotel guests must have thought I was out of my mind.

Twenty-six weeks after we released it, I was out of my mind with excitement and pride as we celebrated a number one single with "That Ain't My Truck," the first of several number ones for newly-activated Decca. To assist us in developing Rhett's fan base, Narvel asked Rhett to open for Reba at Radio City Music Hall in New York City. This allowed our label to fly in radio guests for the appearance, and position our label as a major entity in country music.

In an effort to strengthen our position, our entire staff brainstormed to develop ideas on how we could compete with other major labels. We knew we needed an arsenal of tools to compete. On one occasion, we met at Mark Wright's house and brainstormed connections and ideas that would set us apart, and decided to reach out to a friend of Mark's who worked for the Dallas Cowboys. Through Mark's connection, Decca was able to purchase a suite on the fifty-yard line for four Cowboy home games. We scored four weekends that were ours to use exclusively and we decided to invite groups of key radio personnel in for a game and a musical performance. Each weekend included a day of fun, and evening of music, and a Cowboy game with artists and staff who partied with radio on the fifty-yard line. This was part of our plan to launch Rhett Akins, and launch him we did.

In that first year of operation, we recorded and released singles with Dawn Sears (the most added single by a new artist that year) and Rhett Akins "That Ain't My Truck," as well as a single from Mark Chesnutt "Goin' Through the Big D." Chesnutt's single is particularly memorable. The song played off the words "going through the big D, and I don't mean Dallas," about a guy who was going through a divorce.

During this time period, labels often ran two or three singles to number one in a year with an average chart life of eleven to fourteen weeks. The Chesnutt single was young in chart weeks when we came up against the Christmas break. All charts are frozen for a time during the holidays, and we felt confident the song would be a number one success following the break. We came into the New Year primed to kick it off by celebrating a number one in the first chart week of the year. As stations reported their playlists to *R&R*, the promotion team watched online as we moved between number one and number two. We were fighting it out with Arista's single from Alan Jackson, "Tall, Tall Trees."

Around three in the afternoon we hit number one and held it consistently for the next two hours. Only a few spins separated the two singles, and we held our breath as the clock inched its way toward the chart closing time of five o'clock. The last station to report was a Dallas station, so we felt confident that we had the number one slot guaranteed. After all, how can a Dallas station not report "Going Through the Big D (and I Don't Mean Dallas)?"

We waited and watched. At 5:01, KSCS-Dallas reported their playlist and Chesnutt's single was no longer in the list. The song was showing as a reported drop. Just like that, Chesnutt's single dropped to number two and the Alan Jackson single "Tall, Tall Trees" popped into the number one position. Convinced it was a mistake, we called Lon Helton (chart editor for *R&R*), the music director and program director at KSCS, and left messages at every location we knew to call. It was very convenient for Arista Records that none of the Decca staff could reach any KSCS station personnel until the next day.

The rest is history. We were left with only speculation as to what happened that fateful day. Most of us understand it is the promotion game and someone got to someone. That is the competitive game we play. We were beat at our own game.

Most of that first year was spent hiring and training staff, looking for new talent, finding songs and recording new music for the label. At Fan Fair (now known as the CMA Music Festival) that year, I hosted a luncheon at our Brentwood home for Mark Chesnutt and visiting retail, media, and radio. Lee Adams, who was then at WHYL in Carlisle, Pennsylvania crashed that luncheon, explaining she had heard about it and wanted to meet me. She was apologetic, and stated how much she had always wanted to do label promotion and work for me.

I liked Lee's style and ambition, and I could see she had the tenacity and drive to become a great regional. Over the next few months I thought about her often. When the time came to expand our operation, she was the first and only call I made. One year after meeting Lee in my living room, she became my northeast regional representative. Lee brought a fresh perspective of radio's needs, and a creative approach that blended well into the talent of the other team players. She rapidly became one of my best regionals. Today, she is a vice president of promotion for Broken Bow Records, a strong independent label.

Also at that Fan Fair luncheon, Mark Chesnutt's wife, Tracie, met my dog, Scooter. Scooter was a black and gold Yorkshire Terrier—not a tiny one, but a big old boy who weighed in at around twelve pounds. Scooter was always the life of the party and loved attention, and he reminded Tracie of the Yorkie she had in college. I laughed when Tracie told me how she used to take her dog to class in her book bag.

Unbeknownst to me, when Mark and Tracie returned to their home in Beaumont, Texas, she bought a female that she later bred. She offered one of the two resulting pups to me. Chesnutt's publicist thought we could use the puppy exchange to get publicity for Chesnutt. TNN (The Nashville Network) loved the idea and a press release and teaser campaign started with the tag "Chesnutt Gives the Gift of Love."

Ken and I headed to the Country Music Hall of Fame induction dinner at the Opryland Hotel. Mark and Tracie Chesnutt had a small hotel suite there and we arrived at the suite early. We peered into the bar area that was closed off from the rest of the room. There was a half door and I could see two small black puppies crawling around on the floor. I had told Ken that whichever one came to me on her own was the one I wanted. Secretly, I had my eye on one of them.

The publicist and camera crew arrived shortly after. Once the crew was set up, Chesnutt brought the two puppies out and I sat down on the floor. The one I'd had my eye on turned and began to hop toward me. Scooping her up, I looked into the sweetest eyes I had ever seen and felt my heart melt. We named that baby Stormie Chesnutt Biddy. She graced our home with unconditional love, affection, laughter, and joy for almost sixteen years, and Ken and I loved her more than words can ever express.

At the time, TNN was still on air and had a show called *Music City Tonight* that was hosted by Lorianne Crook and Charlie Chase. *Music City Tonight* did an entire show saluting the new Decca label, and featured both new and established celebrities on the air. Performing that night on June 13, 1994, was Mark Chesnutt, Rhett Akins, and Dawn Sears. Joining me on the couch for talk time was Mark Wright, Owen Bradley (the original GM/producer for Decca) and the legendary Kitty Wells. To top it off, *Country Weekly* covered the gala event with a feature story in their magazine. The press and media attention we were garnering for the label was incredible.

I also saw my beloved Joe Deters retire from MCA in 1994. After years of loyalty, he was pushed out to pasture by corporate powers that believed his time had come and gone. Joe's passion for music and his ear for a hit song were his greatest strengths. While his relationships continued to be strong, the industry was moving toward technology. It was now about managing computer systems and spins. The music business was changing and weaker links were replaced with whatever a company believed would be a stronger link in the future. While it was good for the company, it was sad for me to witness.

Joe's retirement dinner took place that summer in his home city of Atlanta. Artists and staff from across the country paid tribute to the man who had made them stars in his southeastern region. Joe has since passed away, but I know he is somewhere in Heaven making angels laugh with some of the amazing stories he used to tell. I bet he will have a few more to tell me when I get there.

Around this time, Michael began dating a girl he had known from our old Bellevue neighborhood. One day, he told me he wanted to marry again. We talked about the pros and cons, but Michael was confident that this was a choice he wanted to make. Michael was an only child, and I didn't want him to be alone in the world. Like any mom, I wanted him to be loved. He was working at a gutter and home remodeling business and doing his National Guard weekend duty once a month, so I pulled out my first engagement ring and gave it to him. After all, it was the ring his dad had given me and since I had no daughter of my own, I passed it on to him. Michael and Karen married in 1994 and in June 1995, my grandchild Kyle was born. While the marriage was short lived, I am so very thankful for my grandson.

While labels often say they aren't looking to sign any new talent, the truth is a space will magically open if an undeniable voice is presented. In October 1996, the Decca staff was asked to attend a showcase at Cowboy LA Cage, a club in downtown Nashville that has since closed. I liked what I heard of the voice on tape, and was interested to see and hear this young singer in a live performance.

As a staff, we went to a lot of showcases, but it was rare to have a showcase exclusively for one label, or label group, unless the group was paying the cost to showcase. Most publishing companies liked to open the event up to all of the Nashville the labels to see if they could get interest and start a bidding war for their writer/artist.

Lee Ann Womack had been signed to Sony/Tree Publishing. One of her contractual agreements with them was that Sony/Tree would pay for a showcase within one year of her signing her publishing deal. The year was almost up when Lee Ann went to her Sony/Tree writer rep. She reminded them that they owed her a showcase and she wanted to do it for one label: Decca/MCA. This was unheard of. Why would a publisher want to spend money to showcase an artist for one label?

But, Lee Ann knew what she wanted. She told Sony/Tree if they paid for the showcase and she didn't get signed, then she would pay for a second showcase and invite the entire industry. Sony succumbed to her strategy, and most of our staff headed down to Cowboy LA Cage on Broadway to await her performance. Frank Liddell rode with my husband, Ken, and me to the showcase. Lee Ann hit the stage that night in her best Texas attire. She had on jeans, a belt with a big brass buckle, lots of silver jewelry, boots, and some really big hair. She was charming and beautiful, but then the music played and she began to sing. What a voice! I had never heard anything like her. About mid-point in her set, she sang a song called "Never Again Again," And I felt the earth move under my feet.

When the show concluded, Mark Wright and I went backstage to express our interest in Lee Ann. Being from Texas, she had selected Erv Woolsey as her manager (he also managed George Strait). Erv was excited by our enthusiasm, and since several members of the MCA marketing staff had not attended, and MCA provided marketing services for Decca, we asked if Lee Ann would come to our office to play for other key executives.

That next morning, Mark called to schedule a second performance and a meeting inside our A&R offices at Decca. Lee Ann agreed to meet with us about a week later, and brought in several players for her acoustic performance. Our vice president of marketing, Dave Weigand, and our label chairman, Bruce Hinton were also in attendance.

Dave Weigand had replaced Walt Wilson when Walt left MCA for a job at Capitola Records. Dave had worked his way up through the company from a sales rep in Cincinnati, to a country specialist working exclusively for MCA Nashville, to vice president of marketing. By now, the A&R department had grown and moved into the building annex next door. That morning we gathered in Mark's larger office for the performance. Lee Ann brought in an upright base player, a fiddle player, and guitarist. It was the first time we'd ever had an artist perform in our office with an upright bass. They all stood in a semi-circle and sang for those gathered. Once again, Lee Ann's magical voice and performance charmed everyone present, and we offered her a contract.

Interestingly enough, the label had attempted to sign another LeAnn around this time. We‘d heard about a fourteen-year-old singer from Dallas named LeAnn Rimes. Mark had been made aware of her through one of his contacts, and a Mississippi radio station sent a package to me extolling her talents. The Rimes family had lived in Mississippi before moving to the Dallas area.

We began negotiation with her father and then manager, Wilbur Rimes, who also had met with Narvel Blackstock to discuss a possible co-management agreement. Narvel suggested we fly to one of LeAnn's shows in Dallas, and solidify the deal. So, Mark Wright, Bruce Hinton, and I flew down on Narvel's private jet to catch a performance at Johnny High's Country Music Revue in Arlington, Texas.

Afterward, we did everything we could to convince LeAnn's parents to sign with Decca. Later, the family was in Nashville for meetings and we discovered that Mike Curb of Curb Records was also courting her. Mark and I took LeAnn, and her dad and mother, Wilbur and Belinda, to lunch at the Nashville location of Houston's restaurant where we made our best effort to convince them that Decca was the best label home they could have.

During lunch, Wilbur told us what they were looking for in a deal. They wanted to be paid for the one album they had already recorded, and they wanted a draw for the family, since Wilbur would be managing, tour managing, and driving the bus for LeAnn. We said we‘d check with business affairs and get back to them.

Unfortunately, Wilbur also told Curb Records the same thing and Mike Curb instantly said yes. Wilbur liked being directly connected to the decision maker, and Mike Curb didn't have to check with anyone else to give an answer. So, in the end, they decided to sign with Curb Records.

It was only after LeAnn signed to Curb that Ken told me that he had been playing songs for Wilbur and LeAnn. Ken's publishing company, Penny Annie Music, had two songs that LeAnn wanted to cut. When I asked him why he had never told me about LeAnn, he said his chances of getting his songs cut were better at Curb than with Decca, due to politics at our label. He was right. Ken ended up securing two songs on LeAnn Rimes first album, *Blue*. Had she signed with Decca, I can almost guarantee those songs would not have made the album.

Producers have their own publishing relationships and often go to the same songwriters and/or publishers time and again. It is usually because the producer has a percentage of the publishing on a song, or can obtain a piece of the publishing, so they elect to go where they have deals. Mark Wright had been a songwriter signed to EMI Publishing. He once told me that when he left to take the in-house job at Decca, his contract guaranteed that he would cut seven EMI songs per year. I asked how he could be sure that he would find the best seven songs in Nashville at EMI and he said, "Whether they are album cuts or singles, I have always filled my quota." Don't you love this crazy business of music?

LeAnn Rimes's Curb deal was announced soon after we signed Lee Ann Womack. Because LeAnn was under age, we drafted a marketing plan to say we had the "legal Lee Ann" and used her initials, L.A.W., to play off the word *law* with badges and police tape to wrap the marketing plan once it was written. The marketing plan was one of the best we had ever created. We had silver aluminum badges with L.A.W. surrounding the center, fake drivers licenses, fake speeding tickets, and the marketing plan was surrounded by yellow police tape. The plan accomplished what we wanted to with radio, retailers, and press by drawing attention to the music and the uniqueness of the situation. Our plan actually went on to win an industry marketing award.

We decided to release "Never Again Again" as the first single. Even though we were afraid it would polarize with listeners who either loved or hated it due to its traditional sound when it reached the mid-twenties on the chart, we also believed the song would cause people to ask, "Who's that?" And indeed, it did. Once we serviced advances of Womack's music to radio and industry tastemakers, I began to get calls from people who were elated over her talent and the body of her work.

Wade Jessen, who was then music director at WSM Radio in Nashville, called to leave a voice mail message that he had just heard the next "CMA Female Vocalist of the Year," and raved about specific songs on the album. J. D. Cannon at WFMS in Indianapolis called, raving about the songs and which ones he hoped we would release. Alan Jackson called and wanted twenty-six copies so he could have one in each of his houses, boats, and cars. Ronnie Dunn and Vince Gill each called with comments that were wildly enthusiastic about the album and Lee Ann. This is not a natural occurrence. This kind of excitement does not happen often, and when it does, you know you are witness to something powerful. We felt that magic was about to happen.

During Lee Ann's Decca years, she went on to win multiple awards, including the American Music Award, CMA Award, and number one singles and videos with "Never Again Again," "The Fool," and "A Little Past Little Rock." In 1997, *Billboard* named her the #1 New Artist and #1 New Female Artist. She celebrated many firsts in a long line of accolades that spanned decades.

In December of 1994, Mark Wright and I flew to Lubbock, Texas to meet with Mayor David Langston, and tour the Buddy Holly Museum as we began to make plans to record a tribute album to the man himself: Buddy Holly. This project was a brain child of Frank Liddell's, and became a labor of love as Frank discussed artistic options of who should and should not be included in the tribute.

Frank only wanted to include those artists who were influenced by Buddy, and those who were passionate about being on this package. He felt too many tribute projects had artists who were selected to take part in the project solely due to their celebrity, and little on what they brought to a project creatively. He was fiercely protective of this project and evaluated each name thrown on the table to make sure it met his high standards.

The title of the album was *notfadeaway: Remembering Buddy Holly*. The twelve-song album featured a plethora of country and rock talent including Waylon Jennings/Mark Knofler, The Hollies, The Crickets/Nancy Griffith, The Mavericks, Los Lobos, The Tractors, Joe Ely/Todd Snider, Nitty Gritty Dirt Band, Mary

Chapin Carpenter/Kevin Montgomery, Steve Earle/Marty Stuart, and Suzy Boggus/Dave Edmonds.

In addition to the recording of the album, every segment, from the sessions to our marketing meetings, was video-taped as part of a worldwide television special. From that first encounter in December of 1994, it took us two years to record and document all the elements of the project, which was released in January 1996. We were so proud when the album met critical acclaim from the media. The project became a TNN four-hour television special and was celebrated as a #1 Americana Album, Top 5 Triple AAA, Top 5 *Album Network*, and #19 *Billboard* Country Album release. It was selected by *Music & Media* as Album of the Week (the first time a Nashville release had *ever* been selected by this European trade), and the Buddy Holly "notfadeaway" party invitation won an Addy Regional and a National Citation for Excellence award. The label also celebrated a number one video at CMT Europe with the "Well All Right" video with Nancy Griffith and The Crickets.

As I mentioned earlier, Mark Chesnutt was our flagship artist. He graciously took several of our younger artists under his wing and gave them advice. He hosted events where our roster of artists shared the stage and performed their songs at guitar pulls when radio and media was in attendance. One of the purest country voices to ever release music, Mark Chesnutt never got the industry accolades he truly deserved. His career broke the same year as Garth Brooks and Mark often was overshadowed by the success of Garth, Clint Black, Alan Jackson, Travis Tritt, and other male artists who were hugely popular at the time.

With his first four albums platinum, I decided it was time to do something special as a celebration for our flagship artist. When I was growing up there was a popular television show called *This Is Your Life*. In that show, people were honored and surprised by those from their past who showed up as guests to talk about them: an early school teacher, a pastor, a friend, a long lost love, etcetera.

I knew Mark had always dreamed of being a member of the Grand Ole Opry. He told me a story about attending the Opry with his dad when it was still held at The Ryman Auditorium in downtown Nashville. He told the story in an interview, and remembered that he stuck his gum underneath one of the benches on the left hand side. Mark's dad was also a country singer and dreamed of performing on the Ryman stage. He supported Mark in his dreams of pursuing a singing career, but never got to see his son perform at the Ryman.

As I was planning the event, I couldn't think of a more appropriate place to celebrate his success and present his platinum awards than at The Ryman Auditorium. The date was locked in and the Ryman was booked. Plaques were made and everyone was sworn to silence. Mark was told that he was flying in to present an award to Waylon Jennings (a hero of his, and the namesake of his own son, Waylon). We were all hopeful that the night would come off without a hitch, and that our surprise would absolutely be a *This is Your Life* experience.

After Mark arrived at the Ryman and settled in backstage, an escort came to get Mark, and to tell him it was time to present the award. When he stepped onto the stage and the curtains opened, he looked out at an audience who rose to their feet as they celebrated *his* moment and an announcer exclaimed, "Mark Chesnutt this is your life."

A video clip rolled with Mark's childhood photos, and people from his past were ushered out to tell their stories. One by one, a voice shared a story from somewhere backstage and Mark strained to remember the voice. A curtain then opened and a familiar face appeared. A teacher, a long lost friend, his wife, his mother. Each took the stage as Mark wiped tears.

And then, it was our turn to tell the story and present Mark with an award that chronicled over four million records sold. It was a night I will always cherish with love for an artist and a friend who would work with me at three different label imprints.

The Decca Staff in 1994

Loretta Lynn and Lee Ann Womack at a Country Weekly Event

With Jake Kelly and Gary Allan in our Decca Suite at Country Radio Seminar

Between Owen Bradley and Mark Wright (Owen was the original head of Decca Records)

With Helen Darling, Mark Chesnutt, Rhett Akins, Danny Frazier, Mark Wright and Ken Biddy celebrating after CMA Awards

With Bruce Hinton, Mark Chesnutt, Dawn Sears, Mark Wright, Rhett Akins, and Danny Frazier

Rhett Akins impersonating Mark Wright in all his splendor

Ken and I with Rhett Akins, Lee Ann Womack, and Danni Leigh

CHAPTER 13

The Decca Legacy Continues

I was so happy. Never in my life had so many opportunities been presented to me. I was successful at work. I had a beautiful home and entertained often. Ken and I were working hard to build our life together, and we were growing closer as we shared stories of our past lives. We'd visit Atlanta two to four times a year where most of Ken's family still lived. Through Ken, I gained an extended family of brothers and sisters and children whom I came to love and respect. My Mom and step-dad often visited us, and we drove to see them several times a year. While it was often difficult to balance my personal life with work, I did my best to have it all. Life was good.

One afternoon in the summer of 1996, Mark Wright dropped by my office and handed me two cassette tapes that he wanted me to listen to. Both were male artists.

"We can't sign both of these artists," he said, "so I'd like to know which one you like the most."

On my twenty-minute drive from work, I listened to both cassettes, and one voice stood out. The name on the cassette said Gary Allan. Gary had a cry in his voice that comes from a life of experience – a life that understands pain and disappointment. He epitomized the style that we needed to build the Decca label. Mark Wright and I liked the same kind of music so it wasn't a surprise when he said he felt the same way. Byron Hill had produced the tracks, and Byron told Mark Wright that several labels were interested and planning trips to see Gary perform. RCA was going to California the next week to check him out, so Mark said, "We have to get there first."

Byron knew hit songs and voices, and his songwriter efforts paid off with hits recorded by everyone from Johnny Lee with "Picking Up Strangers," to George Strait's "Fool Hearted Memory." By the time he recorded tracks on Gary Allan he had recorded a project with Kathy Mattea, as well as many other artists.

Mark and I quickly headed to Los Angeles. To make it convenient, we booked rooms in a hotel that our MCA chairman, Bruce Hinton, was already at in Century City. Bruce was there for meetings and unfortunately was unable to attend the show at The Crazy Horse in Anaheim that evening. But, he asked that Gary come to his hotel room that afternoon to perform acoustically and Gary obliged.

Gary and his then sidekick, Jake Kelly, showed up right on time and performed several songs. Between numbers, there was the usual chit-chat about musical influences, performance experience, and dreams. I was pleasantly surprised by Gary's charisma and confidence. After Gary's departure from the room, Bruce told us he liked Gary very much, but it was our call. If we liked what we saw with a full band performance, then we had his blessing to move forward with a deal.

In that visit, we learned a great deal about Gary Allan Herzberg. He was born and raised in La Mirada, California to Harley and Mary Herzberg, and to ensure that the family focused on music, Gary's mother insisted that the family's guitars always remain visible in the home.

Like me, Gary grew up quickly, and I have always thought of him as an old soul in a young body. At thirteen, he began to play in honky tonks, with his father. Two years later he was offered his first recording contract from A&M Records, but rejected the deal. Herb Alpert and Jerry Moss formed A&M in 1962 and the offices were on Sunset Boulevard in Los Angeles. The label was a who's who of superstar artists too numerous to mention, celebrating all genres of music. Gary's parents wanted him to finish his education, and his father felt that Gary had yet to develop his own distinctive style. It was a wise parental decision, and one that Gary attributes to his later country success. Despite his commitment to finishing school, he continued to play in bars with his band, the Honky Tonk Wranglers.

Many of the venues they played were packed, and promoters often tried to move Gary to larger clubs. But, the moves would have required him to stop playing older country music, such as covers of George Jones songs, so Gary refused. Gary's respect for classic country music became something I came to respect about this young artist. It was rare to find an artist so young who had such reverence for the musical legends who paved the way.

After Gary's private performance for us, we hopped in a limo for the hour-long drive to the Crazy Horse. This club has always been one of my favorite performance venues. The sound is great and the room is intimate, which allows the audience to sit very close to the stage. When Gary took the stage that evening, he controlled the crowd. His jeans were turned up at the cuff, one fold. His shirt hung loosely on the outside of his jeans, and his cowboy hat was pulled low, shadowing a handsome face and haunting eyes that could see to your soul.

Within the first few minutes, Mark and I both knew we would offer him a deal. When Gary was playing the last song, Mark told me to get Gary as soon as he was through and hold onto him because Dick Whitehouse from Curb was in the building that night. He didn't want Dick to get to Gary before we could meet with him. Dick Whitehouse was an A&R consultant for Mike Curb. He was known to secure deals and had an innate ability to hear talent. He was passionate about music and Mark feared if Whitehouse got to Gary first, it would be over.

I had worked a lot of MCA/Curb acts through the years, and knew Dick had a great ear for a hit song and a hit artist. I knew he would definitely be on the trail, and we did not want to lose another artist to Curb Records, as we had done with LeAnn Rimes. Our work was definitely cut out for us.

A few minutes after the show ended, I grabbed Gary and told him we wanted to offer him a deal.

"Then I'll ask you the same questions I asked all of them," he said. "If I sign to Decca, what would you want to change about me and my music?"

"Nothing," I said. "I love everything I have seen of you on stage and off. I love your look. I love your sound. It's my job to believe in you, and use my talents, abilities, and connections to expose your talent, not to change you into something else. You will evolve in time on your own, as you grow as an artist."

Little did I know, but my answer was the primary reason he signed to our label. Every other label person had answered that question by telling him to lose the cowboy hat, get tighter jeans, tuck in his shirt and "show off that butt."

After we signed Gary, a lot of people talked to me about all the things they thought ought to be changed. I never mentioned one of them to Gary. Artists evolve and change as they grow with success. They don't need label people to direct their every move—unless they ask for direction.

In the limo ride back to Los Angeles that night, I was so excited I called my vice president of promotion, John Lytle. I told him how impressed I was with this young California singer named Gary Allan. John knew that it took a lot to impress me.
"If you are this is excited," he said, "I can't wait to hear him." John eventually left Decca to manage Gary Allan, and continues to represent him today.

With Gary signed to Decca, we began plans to promote and market his release. We loved his music and photo session, but there was one photo of Gary lying across the couch with his boots hanging over one side and his cowboy hat atop the other side where you could not see his face. We loved the photo and wanted it to be the cover for his first CD, *Used Heart for Sale*.

The creative and the marketing departments, however, were not so sure. They reasoned that people would think he was ugly and we had to hide his face. They argued that we needed a face on the CD cover so it would show up in the retail bin. But, no amount of reasoning changed our mind. We wanted to create controversy. We wanted to take a risk, and without risk there is no reward. So the cover stayed, and remains one of my favorites.

We chose "Her Man" as the lead single for Gary's release. Gary's voice was unique, and we felt this song was the perfect one to lead the way. Now it was time to formulate all the elements we needed to secure support from country radio.

One of my favorite radio launch plans was for Gary Allan. With the music recorded and the video shot for "Her Man," we decided it would be easier to take a tour bus to visit radio. The bus would be outfitted with a video screen, state of the art stereo system, and living room where we could bring station personnel on for visits and presentations. We flew into Miami, picked up a Florida Coach, and began our visits, working our way up through the state.

We'd visit one station, perform and maybe have lunch, then board the bus and head to the next station for a performance/visit/meal, and on to the next. By nightfall, we'd be in the city where we had our first morning visit and go to the hotel for some sleep. The driver had to have rest, so we used this opportunity for everyone to get a good night's rest in a hotel bed instead of sleeping on the bus. The next morning, it was early bus call and off to start another day. In between, traveling by bus gave us the opportunity to make calls, check email, and stay in touch with our staff while we continued to introduce Gary to radio.

The times I enjoyed most were those late night drives. Sometimes late at night when everyone had hit their bunks to nap before we checked in, or was in the rear checking emails, Gary came up front to the lounge and visited with me. It was amazing to hear such a young man talk about traditional artists like Johnny Horton, who had influenced his music. Those quiet talks about music, family, and dreams are the takeaways for me. They are the treasured memories I keep inside my heart, and are my personal music business treasures of years and years of late nights and one-on-one conversations.

On that particular bus trip, Ken called to check in, to see how things were progressing, and to find out how Gary was being received at radio. During my conversation with Ken, Mark Wright said, "Let me talk to him." When I handed Mark my cell phone, Ken must have asked him how things were going, to which Mark replied, "Oh, we're just out here hauling Queenie up and down the road." Now that paints a picture, doesn't it?

Decca's success was attracting more artists to our imprint. We were successfully breaking one to two acts a year, and Frank Liddell was pushing for a more diverse roster. For months, he talked of a young Kentucky singer/songwriter named Chris Knight, whom he had signed and developed as a songwriter to Blue Water Music. While Chris's music was stellar, and would most assuredly be a media success with reviewers, we wrestled with how we could position him at radio, and if we could secure any country airplay.

Chris grew up in a mining community in Slaughters, Kentucky, and earned a degree in agriculture from Western Kentucky State University. He taught himself to play guitar at the age of fifteen while listening to John Prine music.

Prine is an American country/folk singer songwriter who moved to Chicago in the 1960s. He was working as a postman, but after hearing some of Steve Earle's music, Prine began to write his own songs. Kris Kristofferson discovered Prine when he performed at a Chicago Folk Festival and got him signed to Atlantic Records where he recorded three albums. Prine later recorded for Asylum and Oh Boy Records, and continues his legacy of music today.

Steve Earle is another eclectic singer songwriter who is a little bit country, a little bit folk, and little bit rock and roll, and his critically acclaimed break-through *Guitar Town* album was released on MCA in 1986. A lot of folk in the Nashville music community loved Steve's music, but couldn't believe we were planning to release singles to country radio. However, Steve's songs "Hillbilly Highway" and "Goodbye's All We Got Left" both reached the top ten on the *Billboard* charts, proving the industry wrong.

Chris Knight adored the music of both Steve Earle and John Prine, but worked for ten years as a mine reclamation inspector, and as a miner's consultant before being offered a label deal with Decca. We were the perfect home for this young Kentuckian who wrote songs from the heart and dreamed of singing them to the world. Chris and Frank lovingly worked on that debut album for over a year.

From the business side I thought they would never complete it. But as we hoped, Chris Knight's 1998 self-titled release met instant critical acclaim. While he celebrated very little country radio success, the release did create a worldwide awareness of his music and his songwriting abilities. He has since become a major name in the alternative country music genre, and is often considered one of the best singer-songwriters to embrace Nashville in the past twenty years. In the years since that release, his songs have been cut by Confederate Railroad, John Anderson, and Randy Travis along with a successful single with Montgomery Gentry called "She Couldn't Change Me."

• • •

I was traveling a lot for work and whenever I called my mom to let her know what I was up to, she would say, "I wish you could stay home. I worry about you on all those planes." I guess we never get too old to be children to our moms. Momma and Dolan grew a garden each year and canned loads of vegetables. Every time we visited, Momma loaded me up with green beans, pickles. relish, or blackberry jam. Regardless of my objections, she insisted I take it all home. Other times, she would say "I got you something," and proceed to pull out a unique item she discovered at a yard sale. My home is filled with those items and those memories: a cookie jar, an oil lamp, a serving bowl. Each one touches me with my mother's love each time I see them. In that way I am reminded every day of her strength and continued love for me.

While Momma and I might be considered strong women by some, many Nashville labels are hesitant to sign female artists because they consider them hard to break and harder to establish credibility with radio and consumers. We were very select in the artists we signed, both male and female. But, there were four great A&R people I was honored to work with throughout my career: Jimmy Bowen, Tony Brown, Mark Wright, and Frank Liddell. Each had the ability to find and hear unique voices, and be able to determine the musical depth of each artist before signing them. It takes so much more than a great voice to be successful in this business.

Many labels today tend to sign females based on their looks, rather than on the depth of their artistry, and then wonder why they have difficulty breaking the act. While we were not always as successful as we hoped, we did sign some incredible female talent who continue their legacy today: Trisha Yearwood, Wynonna, Nancy Griffith, Kelly Willis, and Lee Ann Womack.

In 1997, we were presented another unique opportunity with a young Warner Chappell songwriter named Danni Leigh. Danni had all of the ingredients needed for stardom, including a smoky barroom voice that could reach into your soul. She had a unique look with long blonde hair and a cowboy hat pulled down low. Hailing from the Shenandoah Valley in Virginia, Danni sang traditional country music with a Bakersfield beat and was often referred to as a female Dwight Yoakam.

Michael Knox, son of Buddy Knox and a producer at Warner Chappell, had been developing her sound. Buddy Knox came out with "Party Doll" in 1957 and was the first to write and sing his own number one song in rock and roll. It left an impression on his son and led him into the artist development side of music publishing. Michael Knox produced all of Danni's publishing demos that were later presented to us for consideration. Michael also discovered country superstar Jason Aldean, and has been his producer since the launch of his career. Jason was first signed to Capitol Records in a development deal. Later, when Capitol dropped him from their roster, Michael presented him to Broken Bow's owner, Benny Brown. Benny signed him and Jason opened the door for them to have tremendous label success after a few years of struggling to break an act.

Danni was a perfect fit for a traditional label that had reverence for the sounds of the past, while creating new sounds for the future. Mark Wright and Michael Knox produced her *29 Nights* CD for us while we laid out a huge marketing plan. Her first single "If the Jukebox Took Tear Drops" was released to radio in late summer with an album release in October 1998. The first single was not as successful as we imagined, so we retooled and planned to follow up with the single that radio felt would make her a household name. "29 Nights" was scheduled for a single release in early 1999. Little did we know, but "29 Nights" would never be released.

As often happens, corporations buy other corporations and merge operations. The goal is usually to cut staff and return a profit as quickly as possible. In the summer of 1998, Polygram Records and Universal Music Group, which Decca and MCA were part of, merged. Rumors had been rampant throughout the industry of closures and down-sizing, and all the talk was worrisome to our staff—and to me. We began to receive calls from radio asking how we were doing because they had heard our offices had closed and the lights had been turned off. Regionals called often to see if there was any news. Of course, there had been no announcements or changes.

For almost a year we heard more on the street than we heard internally. It was hard to take care of business and stay focused when I was worried about how long I might be employed. None of us at Decca wanted to look for a new job, because we loved where we were and what we were doing. I was the captain of the ship and didn't feel I needed to be seeking new employment until I knew for sure the status of our operation. As captain, I needed to be the last one to leave the ship.

On January 21, 1999, I was at a Leadership Music Executive Committee meeting that began at eight-thirty that morning. As ten o'clock approached, I turned to our Leadership Music committee chair, Jim Ed Norman, and said, "I have to leave. I have a label meeting that I can't be late for."

The night before, my staff and I had attended a concert at The Ryman for the kick-off of the Crown Royal Tour with Mark Chesnutt, Chely Wright, and Gary Allan. Bruce Hinton and Tony Brown had sat in the row in front of me. All evening they had been evasive, and wouldn't converse or look me in the eye. Something was brewing and I hoped to get some answers.

Each Thursday morning at ten we had a standing Decca recap meeting. Usually Mark Wright and Rick Baumgartner, who was now vice president of promotion, were there. John Lytle had left Decca a year earlier to manage Gary Allan and launch his own company. Rick had been a southwest regional promotion rep for Warner Nashville before he was promoted to a national promotion position at Warner. I hired him away from Warner and made him my vice president.

As we all sat down at the conference table in Bruce Hinton's office, Bruce said, "Today is the day that I clarify the rumors you have been hearing. We are closing Decca Records. Mark, if you and Rick will wait outside, I need to meet with Shelia first, and then I will meet with each of you." Somber, they both rose and as they opened the door to move into the next office, a man I had never seen before entered the room. I was soon informed that he represented the human resources department in Los Angeles, and was there to assist in facilitating my departure.

Lovely, I thought. Fifteen years with the company and it was now to end in five minutes. Even though I wanted it, expected it, clarification is not what I got. The only clarification I got was that I was leaving, and so was most of my staff. Only Mark Wright would be retained, and he would be moved to MCA as an A&R representative. Bruce had always stressed that music corporations value A&R more than any other department personnel.

When I asked which artists were going to be retained, Bruce said he needed to speak with each artist's manager to notify them of the decision before I could be told anything. I felt like an outsider in a home I had built. The locks had just been changed and I no longer had a key.

I could feel my heart beating in my throat as the HR rep explained my separation package, along with the fact that I had only until the end of the day to get my personal belongings and leave. It was chilly in the room, but his words made the room seem a thousand degrees colder. I am sure that HR departments tell executives to keep it short and to the point, to remove emotion, but I needed emotion. I needed to hear that it wasn't my fault. I needed to hear that it was just business. I knew that, but the spoken words I so needed to hear never came.

Thirteen thousand people around the world lost their jobs on that fateful day. Along with the closing of Decca, MCA Nashville and Mercury Nashville were merged into one label. Mark Chesnutt, Gary Allan, and Lee Ann Womack were moved to the MCA roster, and Danni Leigh was dropped from the label, as were Dolly Parton, Chris Knight, and recently signed singer songwriter Shane Stockton.

After I called in my staff and told them the news, I walked next door to Ken's office. His publishing company was in the annex building next door. As I walked in he could tell from my face that I was about to share some troubling news. Together, we had worried about the merger for months. I sat down on the couch in Ken's office and told him about the meeting. Even though Ken is a strong man, I saw the tears well up in his eyes as his composure changed to reflect the agony he was feeling inside. I tried to be strong for him, and also for the staff I had to go back and face.

After I left his office, I stepped into the Decca A&R offices where Mark Wright was sitting at his desk. I asked him if he had told Frank Liddell the news. He told me he had not, that Frank wasn't in the office yet. Then unbelievably, he picked up his phone and dialed a number. "Frank," Mark said, "You need to get your butt to the office. They just closed Decca and you're fired." I could not believe my ears. I shook my head and walked back to my office.

Someone had brought in boxes so I could empty my personal belongings. Someone else copied my computer files and address book so I could take it with me. I am sure they were not authorized to give me those things, but they cared so much for me they did it anyway. As I slowly began to pack boxes, I looked up to see Ken. He sat down at my conference table, and while he did not speak a word, his face spoke volumes. I worried that he would have a heart attack. His heart seemed to be breaking for me.

One by one, MCA staff members from the upper floor stopped by my office to cry and hug me. Fifteen years of dreams were washed away in that merger. But life moves on. Dave Miggo, who worked in our administrative department, came down to my office to see what I needed, to see if he could help. With tears in his eyes, he hugged me then disappeared. He then went outside and took the brass Decca letters off the building and brought them back to me.

"If anyone should have these," he said, "it is you."

This past Christmas, some thirteen years after the label closed, Ken had those letters mounted on a beautiful walnut plaque. They hang in my office today to remind me of the incredible people and artists who came together for several years to accomplish big dreams.

As my staff and I packed away our personal belongings and hidden dreams, none of us wanted to leave. We decided we would go somewhere for an "after doomsday" drink, and gathered at a restaurant that used to be Ireland's Steak & Biscuits on Twenty-First Avenue. We had not been there long when other label people began to show up. The word was spreading along the row and folks were stopping by to pay their regards.

At one point I looked up and saw Danni Leigh running in with tears streaming down her face. She was supposed to be leaving town that night for a string of shows, but was so distraught she didn't think she could do it. "What will I do when they want to introduce me as 'Decca recording artist Danni Leigh?'" she said. I hugged her close and whispered "You will *always* be Decca recording artist Danni Leigh. No one can take that away from you."

As I was leaving, I got a call from Enzo DeVincenzo, who was my now former southwest promotion representative. Enzo had the perfect personality for the job. He was creative and often came up with ideas that made us laugh—and radio loved them, too. Enzo once called to say that he and a promotion rep from another label wanted to rent a motor home and travel through the southwest region visiting radio. Since the two of them were Italian by heritage, Enzo wanted to bill it as "two dago's in a Winnebago." He assured me they would split the cost of the trip between the two labels and split their time talking about records so they both would get equal pitch time. How could I not authorize it?

When Enzo called now, he said he had been fired and rehired in the same afternoon. He had been dismissed from Decca as part of the merger, but Bruce Hinton had called to congratulate him on his new position with MCA doing the same job as he had performed for Decca. Enzo said he didn't agree to work at MCA and wanted my advice.

I knew that Enzo had been offered several high paying jobs while he was working with me. He always told me about them then added that he wouldn't leave me, "If *you* are going down with the ship," he said now, "then *I* am going down with you." I smiled, then told him to make MCA pay him what he was worth. This was his opportunity to collect. If they wanted him, make them pay and make them give him a contract. He followed that advice and worked at MCA several years before leaving to start his own artist management company.

Bruce never called to update me on which artists were being kept or dropped. Dolly Parton read about it in the newspaper. Other artists had to call the label to find out their destiny. It was a dark time around the world, or at least it was for the ones who lost their dreams that day.

Decca Records closed its doors five years and seventeen days after it re-opened. We were billing eight million dollars a year, but it wasn't enough to save the little label against the push of the power brokers. It was a sad day for me—and for the staff and the artists—as we had been the toughest little label to launch in decades.

Bowen always said, "Take care of the music and the music will take care of you." While we did take care of the music, our destinies were changed without any input from us. However, other doors opened when the Decca doors closed.

As I have learned so many times throughout my life and career, we often come to cross roads and are forced to make decisions. Sometimes decisions are made for us, despite our best-laid plans and efforts. When one door closes, another opens and opportunities abound for those who seek them. Like a recording artist or actor, we must all continue to grow and educate ourselves, improve our skills, and seek opportunities to use those skills. Sometimes it is teaching others or consulting, as the younger generation grows into executives, or as singers develop their careers.

The merger at MCA and Polygram was not the last great merger to affect our industry. It seems that every four to five years there is yet another big corporation that vies to buy another big corporation so it can garner more sales and greater chart share. The result is a watershed of talented-displaced executives who are looking for new opportunities.

Never before in the history of Nashville, has there been as many experienced executives available for new opportunities. Many have started marketing, publicity, and promotion companies. Some are now artist managers, while others handle the marketing and radio promotion for independent artists who are thankful to have the resources and connections these people bring to the table.

As a result of the mergers, we are now also seeing an influx of successful independent labels. Many of the key executives from the majors are now heading up the operation of these new entities. In the past thirteen years, we have seen the successful launch of Broken Bow Records and its three label imprints; Big Machine Label Group with its three label imprints: Show Dog/Universal, Streamsound, HitShop; and several others. Their vision is changing the face of the music industry as country's sound evolves, and in this case, change is not necessarily a bad thing.

CHAPTER 14

Life Beyond Labels

A few days after the Decca label closure, an advertisement ran in *R&R* that read in bold print THAT'S NICE with the Decca Records logo below. Many people I knew called the magazine to determine who had purchased the advertisement, but no one was either talking or taking credit for the placement.

There was a joke that circulated around this time about three southern women on a porch sipping mint juleps and discussing all the expensive and wonderful things their husbands had purchased for them on their birthdays and anniversaries. The first two described expensive furs, cruises, cars, and jewelry and continued to brag before saying "But we just keep talking about us. What has your husband given you my dear?"

Having sat quietly through the bragging of the two other women and openly frustrated, the third lady finally declared that her husband sent her to finishing school. "My goodness! That's not a gift! Why would your husband ever send you to finishing school?" one lady boldly asked. The third lady replied, "To teach me to say *that's nice* instead of 'f— you' to women like you." I related with the sentiment completely.

I continued to get a lot of inquiries about the ad. Many industry people thought I had placed it, but I had not. In retrospect, I wish I had. Many months later, when the dust settled, I discovered that one of my employees, April Rider, was the leader of that stealth operation. I love her for doing it, as it perfectly summed up what we were all feeling.

April was passionate about her work. She had developed many of her radio relationships when she was doing independent radio promotion. I hired her as one of my team of regional promotion reps and always believed she would become a vice president of promotion. After the closure of Decca, April went on to serve as vice president of promotion for several labels, as well as general manager for Broken Bow's second imprint, Stoney Creek Records. She soon became very instrumental in the successful launch of that label's debut artist, Thompson Square.

For a year prior to Decca's closing, I had been represented by several high powered attorneys to see what opportunities might be out there for me. With the abounding rumors of the merger, I knew I had to consider all of my options and this was the way the power game was played. These were attorneys who had represented Jimmy Bowen, Bruce Hinton, Tony Brown, Arista Records head Tim DuBois, and Joe Galante, and were considered deal makers. If anyone could cut a deal, these attorneys were the movers and shakers who could make it happen. Alas, nothing surfaced for me, either through their efforts or my own networking.

After about six months, my attorneys, John Mason and Deborah Wagnon, invited me to lunch at the Capitol Grille in downtown Nashville. John wanted to recap his label meetings and give me a status report. After we sat down he looked at me across the table and discussed his frustrations in trying to find me a new label home. "There is not a hairy legged man in Nashville, Los Angeles, or New York who has the credentials or resume that you have," he said. "I hate to say it, but I believe it comes down to one thing, and that is gender."

I was shocked. While I know gender plays a role in the thinking of some executives, I had always tried to not make it an issue. I especially thought it would not be an issue with the upper echelon of executives who made decisions in New York and Los Angeles. John and Deborah both assured me they would continue to take meetings and have conversations, but my "new opportunity" call never came.

Thinking back to the conversation I had with Trisha Yearwood eight years before, I decided to launch my own artist management firm, Shipley Biddy Entertainment. When I told my former boss, Bruce Hinton, what I was planning, he was very encouraging. He said he thought I would be surprised at the caliber of artist who would reach out for representation once the announcement was made.

Danni Leigh reached out first. She had been signed to Decca but was dropped when the merger came down. At the time she had a manager, but she was now at the end of her contractual term and was ready to make a change. I was honored to work with Danni in this new role. It wasn't long before Allen Butler, president of Sony Nashville, reached out to me with regard to Danni. He had been a big believer in her first album and felt his team could bring her the success she truly deserved. He had heard the album, and specifically loved "29 Nights." He felt it was a smash, and considered buying the album master from MCA, or at least the master to that song. When that didn't work out, he decided they would cut a new project.

Sony Nashville signed Danni to their Monument imprint. Strangely enough, I had started my career with Monument Records some twenty-five years before, and now I was managing an artist who was recording for the heritage label. Sony had bought the Monument name some years before from Fred Foster, when he agreed to sell his master recordings. The Dixie Chicks were the second act to be released on Monument and met huge success. Monument had also signed Billy Ray Cyrus, and was planning a release to re-establish him on their label in his post "Achy Breaky Heart" success. All of the label personnel seemed excited about Danni, but several unsuccessful singles later she was dropped from the roster.

Despite the lack of radio success, fans loved Danni and her smoky, traditional-sounding voice. She was featured in magazines from fashion to motorcycles, won European awards, and toured extensively on an international basis.

Soon, Audium Nashville, an independent label, came knocking. Nick Hunter was running the label and had been instrumental in Dwight Yoakam's success when Nick and Dwight were both at Warner Nashville. Nick Hunter had been the vice president of promotion at Warner Nashville. He was also a sports broadcaster and loved baseball, but had left Warner to run Audium Nashville as its general manager. Nick was attracted to Danni's style and felt she was a perfect fit for their operation. Nick signed Danni to Audium and brought in Pete Anderson (Dwight's producer) to produce her new project. The opportunity to work with Pete Anderson was a dream come true for Danni. But again, several failed radio singles ended that deal.

Danni continued to tour in Europe and the United States but felt she could better tap into the Texas market if she moved to Austin. She left Nashville and attempted to work the Texas circuit with moderate success before moving to Spain for a few years in hopes of increasing her overseas exposure. Danni moved back to the United States a few years ago and has a beautiful baby boy. They now live in Virginia, closer to her family.

Another artist I have always loved is Jeff Carson. During my first year in management I attended a Country Radio Seminar and was in the pressroom with Danni, who was doing interviews. I ran into Susan Collier, who handled public relations for Jeff, and Susan introduced me to her artist. Jeff was about to release a new Curb single, but it had been more than three years since his last release. Susan asked if I would take a meeting with Jeff, as he was looking for a new manager. I agreed.

That next week, Jeff and I met to discuss his career. We liked each other immediately, and I began to represent him. My management company and Ken's publishing companies were housed in the same building right off Music Row. The same day I met with Jeff regarding management, Jeff spoke to Ken about a writer deal with his publishing company. Jeff also presented several songs that he could bring to the deal. He had been negotiating with Curb Publishing, but told Ken there was no real interest as it had been over a year since there had been any discussion about signing him as a writer.

Ken loved what Jeff was writing and demoing. He signed Jeff to a publishing deal with his Penny Annie Music company and began to pitch Jeff's songs. Shortly after signing that publishing deal, Ken received a letter from Curb's business affairs people, who were upset that he had signed Jeff. Curb claimed they were trying to sign him to their publishing entity.

When Ken asked Jeff about it, Jeff said no contract was ever issued to him from Curb Publishing—until after he signed with Penny Annie Music. As you will recall, Ken had two songs from his publishing catalog recorded on the LeAnn Rimes *Blue* album. These two songs were high earners for Ken's publishing company, due to the huge worldwide sales of LeAnn's album.

In the same business affairs letter that expressed dismay over signing Jeff to a publishing deal, Curb stated that there were a million albums being claimed as "free goods" on LeAnn's *Blue* album and that his publishing company would not be paid royalties on them. In the music business "free goods" is an incentive offered to retail stores or chains to buy an album. It is often ten free on a hundred, which gives the retailer the ability to make more money if they buy a sizable quantity of product. Whether retaliation or coincidence, it was interesting that both pieces of information were revealed in the same letter.

After three years of waiting for new music to be released, Jeff got the go ahead to record a new project for Curb, and the timing was right for me to get involved as his new manager. Justin Neibank produced an incredible album on Jeff. The single and video for "Real Life" reached top ten on the *Billboard* charts, and fans and industry alike were ecstatic that Jeff Carson was back after a long hiatus.

As was customary, the label planned a CD release party for the music industry journalists. Jeff's party was scheduled for September 11, 2001, and Jeff was going to perform songs from the new CD and do a number of press interviews. All of the Nashville press and radio had been invited, and I was excited for Jeff. Early that morning Ken and I went out for a four-mile walk and returned home about seven-thirty. We walked into our bedroom and I turned on *Good Morning America* while we were getting ready for work. It was then that I saw the news, and watched the planes hit the World Trade Center. Life changed in that moment. The world was never the same.

Jeff's CD release party was cancelled and never rescheduled. The tragedy we faced as a nation was far too painful. A short time later, Jeff Carson and I traveled to New York where he and others performed for the 9/11 first responders at Carnegie Hall. Jeff had always loved the police force and often did ride-a-longs with officers throughout the country. It was a moving tribute to the officers he loved so well, and a memory I will long treasure.

Subsequent singles from that album did not fare well, and Jeff's career once again went into limbo. A manager is only paid a commission if his or her client is touring. Without successful radio singles, it is difficult for an artist to make more than five-thousand dollars a show, and that amount usually goes to pay the band, the bus company, and the booking agent. Often, the artist, the business manager, and the manager are the last to be paid. Without high commissions, I began to dip into my retirement fund to pay the mortgage and keep my little company operational. I made some money, but never enough to cover the full load of business and household expenses.

One afternoon as I was contemplating all this, I received a call from a man named Jeff Huskins who was looking for a vice president of promotion for a new indie label he was launching. He had met with Scott Borchetta and Erv Woolsey, and both had recommended me for the job. Assuming I would not be interested in such a position, he said as much to Scott, but Scott told Jeff he had nothing to lose by asking, and suggested he give me a call. I did not recognize Jeff's name until he explained that he was a former member of the country band Little Texas. He was also a producer who did custom packages for artists who came to town to record projects.

I admit I was a bit leery about working with a former artist who was now a label head and producer, but I agreed to meet with him. The Vivaton Records offices were located in the old Maypop building across from Virginia's Market on 18th and Division Streets. The inside of the offices were beautifully remodeled, the furnishings were expensive, and a flat screen television hung behind the receptionist's desk in the lobby. As I entered the lobby, a sweet, familiar face said hello. Ronna Reeves was staffing the front desk. She had been a Mercury Records recording artist and I had met her several times when I was out socially.

Jeff Huskins was also in the lobby, waiting for me, and seemed very warm. We met for over an hour. He answered all of my questions knowledgably and assured me his investors had 100 million dollars in an account, ready to launch the label. The only hitch was that their daughter was one of the artists signed to the label. That bothered me, but after hearing her voice I felt more confident that we could build a successful operation, despite her relationship to our financial backers.

Jeff outlined my employment package, which included a substantial salary, health insurance for my husband and me, and escalations in salary each year for the next three years. It was apparent that Jeff meant business, as he was paying major label salaries to secure the employees he wanted. I trusted Jeff, and he was ready for me to hire a regional promotion staff even before we had our first artist ready to release. I found I was excited to help him build a successful label. Our promotion staff consisted of Mandy McCormick, Trudie Richardson, Larry Santiago, Brian Thiele, Mara Sidweber, and Tracy Long.

About this same time, Mike Curb agreed to release Jeff Carson. Jeff Huskins loved Jeff Carson's music and was interested in signing him for name value and catalog sales. At the last minute, Becky Judd, Mike Curb's assistant, called to say that Mike wanted to retain the rights to release music on Jeff Carson to the Christian market. He also wanted to release a greatest hits package with new tracks on it.

This was not a good option for us as a start-up label, so we had to walk away from the deal. Once again, Jeff Carson was stuck in career limbo. After a few more frustrating years, Jeff went through the police academy and is now serving on the Franklin, Tennessee Police Force.

I started work at Vivaton on October 1, 2003. Almost immediately, we were in meetings with both Mark Chesnutt and Chely Wright, both of whom I had worked with previously. We had Amy Stevens as in-house counsel and business affairs. Dave Weigand came on, too, as a vice president of marketing. He and I had worked together for fifteen years at MCA and Decca. And, Katie Gillon, who had been our vice president of creative, was now managing Chely Wright. The label quickly came together with these two anchor artist signings. We decided to launch a record from Mark Chesnutt and Chely Wright first, to build catalog while completing our investor's daughter's project. After all, success breeds success and can open the door to break a new artist like Amy Adams.

Jeff Huskins had described our label's investors to me as self-made millionaires who were diversified in a number of businesses. Gregory Setser had been a minister, and had taught churches how to invest their monies to turn a quick profit. Over the years, the Setsers had done so well they had started an import company and were about to go public with their International Product (IPIC) stock. This was in November 2003.

The Setsers, Jeff said, owned a two-hundred-fifty-foot yacht that was anchored outside San Diego, and had offered it to us for radio showcases. They also owned a helicopter, several private jets, a diamond mine in Africa, had offices in Rockefeller Center in New York, and one in London.

It all sounded too good to be true and I asked Jeff if the Setsers were legit. Jeff had apparently hired a Texas investigator to check them out before getting involved and the search could not find anything bad on them. Jeff met the Setsers through their daughter, Amy Adams, who came to Nashville to interview producers for a custom album project. As is often the case, the parents asked Jeff what it would take to start a record label for their daughter. When he explained it was his dream to have his own label, and what it would cost, they agreed to fund it with no strings attached.

Mark Chesnutt's fierce love of traditional music and avid touring schedule was discussed in our initial meetings. Mark wanted to do an album that was a tribute to the honky-tonks he had built his career on. The album was called *Saving the Honky Tonk* and was going to be released on September 24, 2004. Jimmy Ritchie produced that first Mark Chesnutt project for Vivaton.

I had been on the job thirty-nine days when the Setsers and their daughter came into town to attend the CMA Awards. At such a late date, I had to pull every string I had to secure CMA tickets and limos to transport us to the event. After the awards, everyone was hungry, so again, I made a couple of calls. The owner of Valentino's, an upscale restaurant in Nashville, knew me and agreed to stay open for us that evening. We showed up for dinner with bodyguards in tow. I felt it odd that a former preacher would need a bodyguard, but Jeff explained it by saying that Greg Setser carried large sums of cash on him and liked to have security at all times. I guessed that made sense if you considered it that way.

I was excited that Jeff was going to produce Chely Wright's first label project. Although the contract was not fully negotiated, Jeff and Chely were starting to record some tracks at his studio in Gallatin, Tennessee about a little less than an hour north of Nashville. Chely was following him in her car when he got the news that changed everything. The FBI had raided the Setsers California home, arresting everyone in the house and pulling jewelry from their hands as they were led away. This was November 18, 2003 and I had been employed for forty-nine days.

The feds brought down the curtain on what prosecutors and the Securities and Exchange Commission alleged was an elaborate three-year scheme that fleeced evangelical Christians out of one hundred sixty million dollars. We were in shock. Jeff called the staff into his second floor office, and to the best of his knowledge, explained what had happened. We had no knowledge of the scam, nor had we been connected to them contractually.

The FBI met with Jeff Huskins and cleared him of any wrong doing or any knowledge of the Setser's operation. The only helpful thing Jeff could do was provide the offshore account number our payroll was paid from. It was an account number the FBI had been looking for, and details of the account assisted them in processing the case further.

Jeff assured us right away that he would find new investors for our label, and already had a meeting planned with an Atlanta investor through a connection of Katie Gillon's. That connection brought in another Knoxville investor who agreed to fund the company. Both were cleared through the Securities and Exchange Commission and stepped in immediately. Jeff wanted to keep the situation quiet within the Nashville music community, and to my knowledge no one in Nashville ever knew about those investors, or what transpired.

While that transition went smoothly, I realized that Jeff and Chely were having problems. To put it mildly, they were bumping heads. She had more questions than Jeff had answers, so he asked me to go to her Bellevue home and meet with her. He knew she respected me and thought if I explained what had happened with our investors, we could move forward and finish the album.

I drove west to Bellevue, a Nashville suburb, met with Chely, and explained the situation. She had grave concerns but cautiously agreed to move forward with the assurance that we had enough money to successfully launch her project. We planned a single release called "Back of the Bottom Drawer," but it was a rocky process filled with many meetings and disagreements. Finally, she and Katie met with Jeff and me. Neither of us were surprised when she asked for her release from the label, and asked that she be able to buy back her project.

After about a year of money flowing into the label and only one album making it to market, our new investors began to get nervous. In March 2005, I was called into Jeff's office and dismissed. Even though I had eighteen months left on my contract, I was terminated. Next to Jeff I was the highest paid employee, so I figured they were trying to buy some time. Contractually, I was to have thirty days to cure any problem, but that was not to be the case.

After spending eight thousand dollars in attorney fees as I tried to collect my unpaid contractual wages, Vivaton closed its doors in June 2005. The saddest part of the closing: the company left all of its employees out of work and looking for jobs. I believe this company could have been incredibly successful if it had not experienced those early missteps. It had everything, including the executive and musical talent needed for success.

According to online news reports, on January 31, 2007, in Dallas, Texas, Gregory Earl Setser was sentenced to forty years in prison and ordered to pay sixty-two million dollars in restitution for conspiracy, securities fraud, and money laundering. Gregory Setser's sister, Deborah Setser, of Ranch Cucamonga, California was convicted along with Setser and sentenced to fifteen years in prison. Deborah Setser was an officer in Setser's IPIC company, and was involved in the offer and sale of investments in programs with IPIC and Home Recovery Network (HRN), a companion fraudulent scheme also run by the defendants. Cynthia Faye Setser, Setser's wife, did not appear for her sentencing date and remains a fugitive, while his son, Joshua, was sentenced to twenty-four months in prison.

The government contended that IPIC and HRN had no legitimate operations and that its fraudulent operation funded the family's lavish lifestyle and helped maintain the companies' facade. Evidence showed that the Setser's used their ill-gotten gains to buy a $2.3 million yacht, helicopter, several family residences, two small airplanes, and several luxury vehicles. As part of their scheme, they established a website to solicit investors. They also falsely promised investors that their money was at minimal risk, and that they would earn a 25 to 50 percent return on their investment in a three to six-month period. Joshua Setser testified that his father admitted to him that IPIC's ventures were a sham, and that the representations both he and his father made to investors were false.

When all was said and done, it was hard for me to fathom how a person could create a scheme to deceive and defraud so many people of their life savings. I was embarrassed. I had asked all the right questions and gotten all the right answers. While I am not always the most trusting person, I had trusted this situation. Even though I believe Jeff did the best he could to investigate the situation to assure it was solvent, I felt kicked to the curb. I had always strived to be honest in my professional and personal life, and now, artists whom I loved had trusted me with their careers. In addition, former staff members had joined the team in an effort to launch a unique new label imprint. At the time of the closing, I was secretly glad no one in the industry knew what had transpired during those eighteen months of operations, because I was quite ready to move on with my life.

Ken and I joined Jeff and Gina Huskins, Amy and Jason Adams, Greg and Cindy Setser at the Vivaton office prior to CMA Awards

Chely Wright (Center) joined the Vivaton promotion staff. Trudie Richardson and Tracy Long (front) and Mandy McCormick, Larry Santiago, and Brian Thiel (back)

CHAPTER 15

Changes

I am sad to say that my son went through a period of time where he slept in his car and lived in a friend's west Nashville rental home. At first, they had shared the rent, but then the friend moved into a girlfriend's house. Michael lived without water, heat, or air conditioning. Every day, I prayed for God to provide a way for him to survive. Between low wages and child support, his paycheck could not go far enough.

I felt horrible that I could not help him out financially. At the time, I was making no money and was looking for work myself. Our relationship became more strained, when, in frustration, Michael cursed me and wounded me so deeply emotionally that I feared I would never get over the hurt. My new relationship with Michael, or lack of one, was creating havoc with my marriage and cutting holes in my heart. I tried to work and did what I could to be there for Michael, even if it was in spirit only.

After Vivaton closed, I secured my real estate license in 2005. I returned to Hallmark Direction Company, continuing to sell real estate while I managed artists for Hallmark. Real estate, I found, was an expensive and time-consuming process. I love that industry and hope to return to it one day, but I love the music business more and was not ready to walk away from it.

So instead, at two different companies, I managed artists. At Shipley Biddy Entertainment I managed Danni Leigh, Jeff Cason, and the band Alvarado Road Show; and at Hallmark Direction Company I managed Trent Willmon, Ray Scott, The Parks, Flynnville Train, and Jaclyn North. I also assisted in the launch of Stringtown Records for John Michael Montgomery.

In late 2010, I got a call from my mother that my step-dad had suffered a stroke. I rushed to the hospital to see him and was so glad that he recognized me. He grabbed my arm and squeezed it as I told him I loved him. He was moved to a nursing facility a few weeks later and died on December 26, 2010. The last few years have been hard on Momma as she works to keep up her property.

She regularly mows the yard and still raises a garden. In 2013, (the year she turned eighty) she broke her hip when she was dragging cornstalks to the pasture for the goats to eat. Momma is such an amazing woman. She was walking on her own the day after surgery and refused rehab. Then, she threw her walker away after two weeks because she said it made her look old. Talk about a strong woman!

Michael has also turned out to be a strong member of our family. He remarried two years ago to a girl named Kimberly Lane, who he had known since grade school. Together, they are raising Kim's daughter, Kate. He now lives in Scottsville within a mile of my Mom. He is working hard at a job he loves and goes to church each Sunday. Prayers do get answered so never give up. The wound in my heart is finally healing. I am so thankful to have them in my life.

By 2009, many of the top level artists who had been managed by Hallmark, had changed managers and left the company. Hallmark had downsized to three employees. John could no longer make payroll and we were acting as if it was business as usual while looking for new employment. It had been two years without a paycheck. I was frustrated beyond frustrated and terrified that I would lose everything Ken and I had worked to achieve. Through the years I have had several industry executives suggest that I start my own independent promotion company. Knowing how deeply I get involved, and how frustrated I get if things don't work out the way I planned, I never thought I would consider doing freelance radio promotion when I read about the launch of a new company that sounded intriguing.

In April 2011, a press announcement stated that entertainment attorney Nancy Eckert and booking veteran Louis Newman had announced the formation of Flying Island Entertainment, a Nashville-based artist service company designed to address the needs of both new and established country artists. The article went on to say that Nancy Tunick of Grassroots Promotion would oversee the staffing of Flying Island's radio division, and serve as its label and promotion consultant. Tunick would also continue in her role as managing partner and co-owner of Grassroots Promotion.

Excited, I went online and researched Nancy Eckert, as that was a name I did not know. I was impressed with her credentials and the services she provided at another company she owned called Verge. The only Louis Newman I knew was a southeast regional rep for MCA Nashville. He spelled his name differently and I knew he had never done booking, so this Louis also proved to be someone I had not met before.

I did know Nancy Tunick, however, so I reached out to her to make her aware of my interest. When she returned my call, she seemed surprised that I would consider doing regional promotion for a new indie company. I assured her I was indeed interested, and we discussed the Midwest region. I did my homework and prepared a list of all of the radio programmers within the region that I had a current relationship with. I did everything I could to prep for a meeting, should one be granted.

It was several weeks and several voice mails later to both Nancy's before I finally got the call for an interview. I had almost given up hope of getting that call, and thought they did not want to consider me for the position. After all, I had reached out to most of the major and independent labels and offered to do regional promotion or radio marketing, only to be turned away without an interview.

I liked Nancy Eckert right away. She had an outgoing personality and was extremely knowledgeable about the industry. Once Nancy Tunick got there, we had an exciting conversation about radio promotion and the changes within our industry. They caught me up on Flying Island's artist, Gwen Sebastian, and said the team would also take on select outside clients for radio promotion. I was offered the job on the spot, but it was during that meeting that my regional assignment changed. I was hired to handle the east coast territory for Flying Island, covering radio from Maine to Miami, and I was proud to have it.

I am so glad I had the opportunity to be a regional for Flying Island. It gave me a whole new perspective of what my own regionals experienced for so many years. It is a tough life out on that road. There is a lot of hard work and many lonely hours in every one of those road trips. I have much more empathy for each of them now. I will also say that it is a lot harder to confirm travel when you work for an indie label than it was when I worked for

MCA or Decca. While I still have a lot of friends in radio that I have known for thirty years, many of the new programmers had no idea of my background.

For eighteen months, I handled the east coast. As an independent company, we did a lot more driving than flying, in an effort to hold down the cost for the client. My longest drive was from Atlantic City, New Jersey to Portland, Maine. It took almost twelve hours, due to rain and toll roads. By the time we reached the hotel in Portland, my hands were so sore I could barely unbend my fingers, my legs hurt, and my eyes stung from the strain of watching the road. It took a second trip to the northeast before I was told about a toll pass that could be obtained for the rental cars. That was a time saver I was glad to discover.

Jill Tomalty was the rep who was hired for the Midwest region. She was originally from Michigan, so I am sure this was the reason why the territory was assigned to her. In January 2013, when I was named president of Flying Island, Jill inherited my eastern stations as we redefined territories. I am much more of a numbers person, while Jill is more of a personality. She easily stepped into her new-found responsibilities and worked hard to develop relationships.

In March 2013, Dan Matthews joined us for West Coast duties and fit in nicely to the Island family. He was young and aggressive, and while his experience was primarily in radio, when he moved to the promotion side he said he should call all the reps back and apologize for not taking or returning their calls when he was in radio. Payback can be painful. Working at a small label, programmers can easily write us off. They get so many calls that they favor the majors, who have more bargaining power and marketing dollars to spend.

Bonita Allen was the cement that held us together. She was hired as our promotion manager but she took on new roles daily. She handled all of our classic country media interviews and edited them as part of our servicing to radio. She also did radio promotion to the *Music Row* reporters and juggled e-blasts and reports with a smile on her face. I finally felt at home again with a family of passionate and caring people. Every day was a wonderful day on The Island.

We were thrilled when our flagship artist, Gwen Sebastian, appeared on the second season of NBC's *The Voice*. While it delayed our single launch, it also secured Gwen a position in Blake Shelton's band singing background vocals on his tour.

We spent seven months on the road visiting radio and doing shows across the country. In between Blake's tour, Gwen performed her own shows. By the fall of 2012, Gwen had been named one of *Country Weekly's* Top 10 Most Beautiful Women and had opened for Miranda Lambert and Dierks Bentley on some east coast shows. Gwen performed in front of seventy-thousand people at the Titans Stadium during CMA Music Fest 2012 and appeared several times on the Grand Ole Opry. In 2013, we launched a new single, "Suitcase," as well as a release of a fifteen song self-titled CD distributed by Warner Nashville.

We were proud of what we accomplished for Gwen. We often laughed in our meetings and commented that, "we are small, but we are loud." In becoming president of Flying Island I was honored that Nancy Eckert, Louis Newman, and our investors felt confident in my abilities to lead us into a new phase of growth. We continued to be innovative in our approach to launching new talent, while paying attention to the legends of our format with our classic country media service. After all, many of the artists I worked with from the eighties to the nineties are now considered classic artists, and are played on classic country radio stations.

While Flying Island was funded by investors, it needed to secure paying clients to cover payroll expenses. The financial investment was primarily in support of Gwen Sebastian. By the summer of 2013, however, it was apparent that the climate was changing. Fewer clients could afford to hire us, and Gwen's album was not selling well. The lead single from the album was not being received as well as the previous single, and everyone was getting antsy. On September 3, the operation was shuttered and the promotion staff dismissed. Once again, I found myself wondering where I would land. I prayed the right door would open. It did.

As soon as the announcement of Flying Island's closing was made in the trade magazines, I got a call from Tatum Hauck Allsep. Tatum is an honors graduate from Vanderbilt University who spent six years at MCA, beginning as an intern and working her way into the promotion department. After leaving MCA,

Tatum managed the Americana band, The Derailers, and later launched the first-ever Vanderbilt Medical Center / Children's Hospital Music Industry Relations Department.

During her years with Vanderbilt Medical Center, Tatum was instrumental in the launch of several programs including Dierks Bentley's Miles and Music for Kids, Project Paper Doll, Musicians on Call, and Music Heals Campaign. When she left Vanderbilt, she co-founded a for-profit company called Sound Healthcare, which was an expansion of the Country Music Association's program that provided health insurance and advocacy for members of that trade organization.

The experience gave Tatum a first-hand look into the growing need for a full service healthcare advocacy firm to protect and serve the music community, so she formed a non-profit called Music Health Alliance. This new model of healthcare advocacy removed the profit motive from the insurance model, while providing healthcare options for a group of people she had always loved: musicians, singers, songwriters, and behind the scenes supporters of music.

Tatum informed me that Kimberly Sexton Dunn was working with her as well. Kimberly had worked at MCA as a promotion regional. And, Herky Williams had joined Tatum and Kimberly as director of development. Since we would be funded exclusively by donations and fund-raising, Herky would be critical to the nonprofit's financial solvency since we were dependent up donations and fund-raising to cover payroll and expenses. I knew Herky from his years with ASCAP, and when he worked for Jimmy Bowen. It was a small world indeed.

Tatum wanted to talk to me, so we scheduled a meeting for the following week. I was excited, and hoped the meeting could lead to my involvement with the organization. I did a lot of online research about advocacy and navigation, two new terms in healthcare that I was unfamiliar with. When I sat down with Kimberly and Tatum, they told me stories of how they had saved six families from bankruptcy in the ten months they had been in operation. They had negotiated the write-off of hundreds of thousands of doctor and hospital bills from music industry veterans who had no health insurance, or who had errors in their billing.

They also assisted people in getting free prescriptions and doctor's care when they could not afford it. Completely confidential, they were helping so many music industry people navigate their way through troubling times. I was in awe. This was a whole new world. My volunteer work had always been on music industry boards. While I wanted to do good for other people, my do-gooding always seemed to be work related. As I listened to these stories, I knew I wanted to be part of this new entity. I had prayed about it and read about it, and talked to Ken for a week hoping there was a place for me.

Then, Tatum shared her own personal story. She talked about praying over her decision to meet with me. She prayed for an answer and wanted to know if hiring me was right for the team — right for where they were in the launch of this new company. Her answer was "yes." While she was not financially able to offer me what I had been earning, she wanted me to join their team as director of operations.

"It may be a bit earlier in the timeline than I would have wanted," she said, "but you bring the organizational skills we need. You have launched successful companies. I watched you at MCA and Decca overcome obstacles that would have made others stumble, and you always survived. While the timing might not be right financially, I need you now. I *know* the timing is right."

Tatum described how everyone was on half wages until we received funding. No press announcement had been circulated, because they wanted to build their success story before announcing the company. I had considered options in the healthcare industry but did not know where to start. Now I was being offered an opportunity to take my organizational and people skills to assist those in the music industry I loved that needed help. I did the math and knew I couldn't live on that half salary, but I also knew that Tatum believed in what she was doing—and in me. I, too, believed in what she was doing.

I studied, and got my license to sell health insurance. I sweated bullets studying for that exam. The days leading up to the test seemed to drag by. Finally, on a Friday night at five-thirty in the evening, I entered the exam room. Seventy minutes later I exited and was handed a slip of paper that showed that I passed. In the months to come, I will study and grow and hopefully become an expert in Medicare and all of the advantage and supplemental plans.

In the past year, I have worked as an advocate for so many people who are suffering with cancer and from the debt of medical bills that bury them while they fight their fight. I am humbled at the need and thankful that God has given me the opportunity to serve these new friends. At sixty two years of age, I feel like a ship that is just being launched for the first time. Who knows what lies around the bend in the river or across the next horizon? As Tatum says, "We are building a legacy that will live on long after we are gone." That's a very nice thought.

As a nonprofit, Music Health Alliance depends on the philanthropy of individuals, foundations, grants, and fundraising events. This year, Gibson Guitar partnered with Music Health Alliance making them the charity partner for their Tribute To Southern Rock Guitar resulting in a donation of $107,000. It was the largest donation to date. I hope they know just how much good is being done with those funds and how many lives are being changed on a daily basis.

My music industry career began with an independent label, Monument Records, and after several stints with the major labels, I am once again at the helm of an independent thinking company. This time it is a company that can help others in entertainment with their most critical health needs. Once, long ago, Fred Foster made a call to a doctor that saved my life. Thirty-seven years have passed since that day. Now, I am thrilled that I can reach out and say, "Can I help you?"

For anyone who is at a crossroad, remember that left or right can both be correct answers. Choose left and it will take you down one pathway. Choose right and it takes you another way. Make the best decision you can at the time and see where destiny takes you. Just remember, you are in control of your decision each and every time. No one else can make that decision for you.

In my career, I have experienced success and grandeur beyond anything I could have dreamed. I have flown in private jets with Reba McEntire and Brenda Lee. I've known the comfort of private car service in New York and Los Angeles. I have stood backstage at Carnegie Hall, Radio City Music Hall, Broadway musicals, symphony stages, and arena stages nationwide. I've met with film producers in Hollywood and stood backstage at the Hollywood Bowl. I have danced in the Rainbow Room in New York City, and sat with friends in the Sears Tower overlooking Chicago as the sun set. I have known the highs of success and the lows of failure. I have made dreams come true and seen dreams shattered. I have had someone weak with cancer thank me for being there and for providing help when they most needed it. If I had decided to leave Monument so many years ago and take that television job, how different would my life have been? Did I change the music industry? Did I make a difference in the lives of the people who worked for me? Did I help the artists whose careers we launched? Did I help make dreams come true? I hope so. I really do.

I have been blessed with an incredible career. But along with the success came personal sacrifice, time away from family, too much work and often too little play. The personal sacrifice was not always mine. I was not always able to be there as a wife or mother or grandmother when the people I loved needed me. I tried to balance life and work as much as possible, but often work won out. At the end of the day, I hope my family knows how much I love them. I could not have accomplished my dreams without their continued support. Would I do it all again if given the opportunity? You bet I would. Who knows? Maybe the best is yet to happen. I am confident that there are many more crossroads before I sleep. I definitely plan to add more music in my rearview mirror before it is time to say goodbye.

—The End—

Michael and Kimberly Shipley and my Mom on their wedding day in August 2012.

John Dorris and I with The Parks (Johnny & Clint) at their label Christmas party

ABOUT THE AUTHOR

Shelia Shipley Biddy is one of the most respected women in the music business. Her achievements span four decades and include a bevy of ground breaking career choices and numerous awards and recognitions.

Biddy was *Mirabella Magazine's* Reader's Choice "1000 Women For The Nineties." She was voted *Gavin Magazine's* Country Promotion Vice President of the Year on three occasions and *Nashville Life Magazine* voted her one of "Nashville's Top 25 Most Influential Women." She was selected as one of the top career women in the music industry for *Billboard's* book, *Women at the Top,* and included in the 1998 edition of the *Country Music Hall of Fame's Encyclopedia of Country Music."*

She was presented with the CRB (Country Radio Broadcasters) President's Award in March 2009, which recognized her significant contribution to the marketing, production, growth and development of the Country Radio Seminar, and the multiple services that Country Radio Broadcasters provide to the country radio and music communities. In 2012, she was inducted into the SOURCE Hall of Fame, an organization she co-founded in 1991. SOURCE is a nonprofit organization that supports women executives and professionals who work in all facets of the Nashville music industry.

Shelia Shipley Biddy lives with her husband Ken Biddy just off Nashville's Music Row.

www.sheliashipleybiddy.com
www.Facebook.com/SheliaShipleyBiddy
www.Facebook.com/TheMusicInMyRearviewMirror
Twitter: @SSBiddy

"Commit your work to the LORD, and your plans will succeed." Proverbs 16.3

ADDENDUM A

SHELIA SHIPLEY BIDDY'S CAREER NUMBER ONE SINGLES

Year	Artist	Title	Label	Weeks At # 1
1984	George Strait	You Look so Good in Love	MCA	1
1984	Don Williams	That's the Thing About Love	MCA	3
1984	George Strait	Let's Fall to Pieces Together	MCA	1
1984	George Strait	You Look so Good in Love	MCA	1
1984	Don Williams	That's the Thing About Love	MCA	3
1984	Jim Glaser	You're Getting' to Me Again	MCA	1
1984	John Conlee	In My Eyes	MCA	1
1984	John Conlee	As Long as I'm Rockin' With You	MCA	1
1984	Don Williams	Stay Young	MCA	2
1984	Barbara Mandrell	Happy Birthday Dear Heartache	MCA	1
1984	George Strait	Right or Wrong	MCA	1
1984	Lee Greenwood	Going Going Gone	MCA	1
1984	Oak Ridge Boys	I Guess it Never Hurts to Hurt Sometimes	MCA	2
1984	Oak Ridge Boys	Everyday	MCA	2
1984	John Schneider	I've Been Around Enough to Know	MCA	1
1985	George Strait	Does Fort Worth Ever Cross Your Mind	MCA	4
1985	Reba McEntire	How Blue	MCA	1
1985	Oak Ridge Boys	Make My Life Without You	MCA	2
1985	Kenny Rogers	Crazy	MCA	1
1985	Bellamy Brothers	I Need More of Your Love	MCA/ Curb	1

1985	Lee Greenwood	You've Got a Good Love Coming	MCA	1
1985	John Schneider	Country Girls	MCA	1
1985	Reba McEntire	Somebody Should Leave	MCA	2
1985	Oak Ridge Boys	Little Things	MCA	1
1985	Lee Greenwood	Dixie Road	MCA	2
1985	Oak Ridge Boys	Touch a Hand, Make a Friend	MCA	2
1985	Bellamy Brothers	Lie to You for Your Love	MCA/ Curb	1
1985	Steve Wariner	Some Fools Never Learn	MCA	1
1985	Lee Greenwood	I Don't Mind the Thorns (When You're the Rose)	MCA	1
1985	George Strait	The Chair	MCA	1
1986	Steve Wariner	You Can Dream of Me	MCA	2
1986	Oak Ridge Boys	Come on In	MCA	1
1986	John Schneider	What's a Memory Like You (Doing in a Love Like This)	MCA	2
1986	Lee Greenwood	Don't Underestimate My Love for You	MCA	1
1986	Bellamy Brothers	Feelin' The Feelin'	MCA/ Curb	2
1986	Reba McEntire	Whoever's in New England	MCA	1
1986	Lee Greenwood	Hearts Aren't Meant To Break	MCA	2
1986	Steve Wariner	Life's Highway	MCA	1
1986	George Strait	Nobody in His Right Mind Would've Left Her	MCA	2
1986	John Schneider	You're the Last Thing I Needed Tonight	MCA	1
1986	Reba McEntire	Little Rock	MCA	2
1986	Bellamy Brothers w/ Forester Sisters	Too Much is Not Enough	MCA/ Curb	1
1986	George Strait	It Ain't Cool to Be Crazy About You	MCA	1

1987	Reba McEntire	What am I Gonna Do About You	MCA	1
1987	Lee Greenwood	Mornin' Ride	MCA	1
1987	George Strait	Ocean Front Property	MCA	1
1987	Steve Wariner	Small Town Girl	MCA	1
1987	Bellamy Brothers	Kids of the Baby Boom	MCA/ Curb	1
1987	Waylon Jennings	Rose in Paradise	MCA	1
1987	Oak Ridge Boys	It Takes a Little Rain	MCA	1
1987	Conway Twitty	Julia	MCA	1
1987	George Strait	All My Ex's Live in Texas	MCA	1
1987	Reba McEntire	One Promise Too Late	MCA	1
1987	Steve Wariner	The Weekend	MCA	1
1987	Oak Ridge Boys	This Crazy Love	MCA	1
1987	Bellamy Brothers	Crazy From the Heart	MCA/ Curb	1
1987	George Strait	Am I Blue	MCA	1
1987	Steve Wariner	Lynda	MCA	1
1987	Reba McEntire	Let the Music Lift You Up	MCA	1
1987	Reba McEntire	The Last One to Know	MCA	2
1987	Steve Wariner	Lynda	MCA	1
1988	Desert Rose Band	One Step Forward	MCA	1
1988	George Strait	Famous Last Words of a Fool	MCA	1
1988	Reba McEntire	Love Will Find it's Way to You	MCA	1
1988	Desert Rose Band	He's Back and I'm Blue	MCA	1
1988	George Strait	Baby Blue	MCA	2

1988	Patty Loveless	A Little Bit in Love	MCA	1
1988	Oak Ridge Boys	Gonna Take a Lot of River	MCA	1
1988	Desert Rose Band	Summer Wind	MCA	1
1988	Reba McEntire	I Know How He Feels	MCA	2
1989	Desert Rose Band	I Still Believe in You	MCA	1
1989	Reba McEntire	New Fool at an Old Game	MCA	1
1989	George Strait	Baby's Gotten Good at Goodbye	MCA	2
1989	Steve Wariner	Where Did I Go Wrong	MCA	1
1989	Reba McEntire	Cathy's Clown	MCA	1
1989	George Strait	What's Going on in Your World	MCA	1
1989	Patty Loveless	Timber I'm Falling in Love	MCA	3
1989	George Strait	Ace In the Hole	MCA	1
1990	Patty Loveless	Chains	MCA	2
1990	Oak Ridge Boys	No Matter How High	MCA	1
1990	Reba McEntire	Walk On	MCA	1
1990	Patty Loveless	On Down the Line	MCA	1
1990	George Strait	Love Without End, Amen	MCA	5
1990	Vince Gill	When I Call Your Name	MCA	1
1990	Reba McEntire	You Lie	MCA	1
1990	George Strait	I've Come to Expect it From You	MCA	5
1991	Reba McEntire	Rumor Has It	MCA	1
1991	Mark Chesnutt	Brother Jukebox	MCA	2
1991	Vince Gill	Pocket Full of Gold	MCA	1
1991	Mark Chesnutt	Blame it on Texas	MCA	1
1991	George Strait	If I Know Me	MCA	2

1991	Trisha Yearwood	She's in Love With the Boy	MCA	2
1991	George Strait	You Know Me Better Than That	MCA	3
1991	George Strait	If I Know Me	MCA	2
1991	Lionel Cartwright	Leap of Faith	MCA	1
1991	Mark Chesnutt	Your Love is a Miracle	MCA	1
1991	George Strait	The Chill of an Early Fall	MCA	1
1991	Trisha Yearwood	Like We Never Had a Broken Heart	MCA	1
1991	Conway Twitty	I Couldn't See You Leavin'	MCA	1
1991	Reba McEntire	For My Broken Heart	MCA	2
1992	Reba McEntire	Is There Life Out There	MCA	2
1992	Wynonna	She is His Only Need	MCA/ Curb	1
1992	Vince Gill	Take Your Memory With You	MCA	1
1992	McBride & The Ride	Sacred Ground	MCA	1
1992	Trisha Yearwood	The Woman Before Me	MCA	1
1992	Wynonna	I Saw the Light	MCA/ Curb	3
1992	Mark Chesnutt	I'll Think of Something	MCA	1
1992	Vince Gill	I Still Believe in You	MCA	2
1992	George Strait	So Much Like My Dad	MCA	1
1992	Wynonna	No One Else on Earth	MCA/ Curb	4
1992	Reba McEntire	The Greatest Man I Never Knew	MCA	1
1992	Vince Gill	Don't Let Our Love Start Slippin' Away	MCA	3
1992	McBride & The Ride	Going Out of My Mind	MCA	1
1992	Trisha Yearwood	The Woman Before Me	MCA	1

1992	George Strait	I Cross My Heart	MCA	2
1992	Wynonna	I Saw the Light	MCA/ Curb	3
1993	Wynonna	My Strongest Weakness	MCA/ Curb	1
1993	George Strait	Heartland	MCA	1
1993	Reba McEntire and Vince Gill	The Heart Won't Lie	MCA	2
1993	Reba McEntire	It's Your Call	MCA	1
1993	Vince Gill	No Future in the Past	MCA	1
1993	Mark Chesnutt	It Sure is Monday	MCA	1
1993	Tracy Byrd	Holdin' Heaven	MCA	1
1993	Wynonna	Only Love	MCA/ Curb	1
1993	George Strait	Easy Come, Easy Go	MCA	2
1993	Wynonna	Tell Me Why	MCA	1
1993	Vince Gill	One More Last Chance	MCA	1
1993	Mark Chesnutt	Almost Goodbye	MCA	1
1993	Reba McEntire w/ Linda Davis	Does He Love You	MCA	1
1994	George Strait	I'd Like to Have That One Back	MCA	1
1995	Mark Chesnutt	Going Through the Big D	Decca	1
1995	Rhett Akins	That Ain't My Truck	Decca	1
1995	Mark Chesnutt	Gonna Get a Life	Decca	1
1996	Rhett Akins	Don't Get Me Started	Decca	1
1997	Mark Chesnutt	It's a Little Too Late	Decca	3
1997	Mark Chesnutt	Let it Rain	Decca	1

1997	Gary Allan	Forever and a Day	Decca	1
1997	Lee Ann Womack	The Fool	Decca	1
1998	Lee Ann Womack	A Little Past Little Rock	Decca	1
1998	Mark Chesnutt	Thank God for Believers	Decca	1
1999	Mark Chesnutt	I Don't Want to Miss a Thing	Decca/ MCA	5
1999	Lee Ann Womack	I'll Think of a Reason Later	Decca/ MCA	2

ADDENDUM B
DECCA MILESTONES

1994

Most Added Debut Female Artist Ever *in Gavin Magazine* with Dawn Sears - 104 Adds
June TNN Special featuring Decca Executives and Artists
Decca Label ranked #14 "Singles Label" in year-end *Billboard* chart analysis
Mark Wright #9 *Billboard's* "Hot Singles & Tracks Producer"

1995

Mark Chesnutt ranks #18 and Rhett Akins ranks #44 for "*Billboard's* Hot Country Singles & Tracks Artists"
Mark Chesnutt ranks #32 for *Billboard's* "Top Country Artists"
Mark Chesnutt "What a Way To Live" album certified Gold
Rhett Akins ranks #7 for *Billboard's* "Top New Country Artists"
Rhett Akins ranks in *R&R's* Top New Artists to break inside Top 15
Rhett Akins voted by radio as *R&R's* "New Artist MVP" at #10
Rhett Akins *R&R's* "Most Played Song of the Year at #10 for "That Ain't My Truck"
Rhett Akins *Network 40's* "Most Played Song of the Year at #2 for "That Ain't My Truck"
Rhett Akins *Gavin's* "Most Played Song of The Year at #29 for "That Ain't My Truck"
Rhett Akins #1 in *Gavin* with "That Ain't My Truck"
Rhett Akins #1 video at CMT with "That Ain't My Truck"
Rhett Akins is selected by *Country America* as Top 10 Best New Artist For 1995
Mark Chesnutt #1 *Gavin* with "Goin' Through the Big D"
Mark Chesnutt #1 *Billboard, R&R,* and *Gavin* with "Gonna Get a Life"
Mark Chesnutt #1 video with "Gonna Get a Life"
Mark Chesnutt ranked #42 for *Billboard's* "Top Country Album Artists"
Mark Chesnutt ranked #15 in *Gavin* with "Gonna Get a Life" and #44 for "Goin' Through the Big D"
Mark Chesnutt ranked #15 as Most Played Gold Artist in John Hart Media research for year end
Decca Label ranked #13 for "Top Country Labels" and #13 for "Top Singles and Tracks Label"
Mark Wright is ranked #8 *Billboard's* "Hot Singles & Tracks Producer"
Shelia Shipley Biddy voted as "Top 20 Most Influential Women in Nashville by *Nashville Life* readers"

1996

Buddy Holly *notfadeaway* four-hour television special, #1 Americana Album, Top 5 Triple AAA, Top 5 *Album Network*, and #19 Billboard country album release
Buddy Holly *notfadeaway* album selected by *Music & Media* as Album of the Week (the first time a Nashville release has *ever* been selected by this European trade)
Buddy Holly *notfadeaway* party invitation wins ADDY Regional and National Citation for Excellence Award
#1 CMTE Video with "Well All Right" video with Griffith & Crickets
CMT Europe "Video Event of the Year" Award for Nanci Griffith and The Crickets for "Well All Right" video
Mark Chesnutt #68 *Billboard's* "Most Played Song All Musical Formats"
Mark Chesnutt #26 *Billboard's* "Most Played Artists of the Mid 90's (1995-1996) All Formats"
Mark Chesnutt "It Wouldn't Hurt to Have Wings" #42 in Billboard's "Top 100 Country Singles & Tracks)
Mark Chesnutt #40 in *Billboard's* "Country Singles & Tracks Artists"
Mark Chesnutt #2 *in Network 40's* "Top 100 Most Played Songs" with "It Wouldn't Hurt to Have Wings" (98,475 detections)
Mark Chesnutt #33 in *Gavin's* "Top 150 Songs" with "It Wouldn't Hurt to Have Wings"
Rhett Akins "Don't Get Me Started" #34 *in Billboard's* "Top 100 Country Singles & Tracks)
Rhett Akins nominated as American Music Award's Best New County Artist (only three artists in category)
Rhett Akins #36 in *Billboard's* "Country Singles & Tracks Artists"
Rhett Akins #50 in *Billboard's* "Top Country Album Artists"
Rhett Akins #16 in *Network 40's* "Top 100 Most Played Songs" with "Don't Get Me Started" (90,352 detections) and #95 with "That Ain't My Truck" (55,964 detections)
Rhett Akins #14 in *Gavin's* Top 150 Songs with "Don't Get Me Started" and #99 with "That Ain't My Truck"
Rhett Akins #1 in *R&R*, *Network 40*, and *Gavin* with "Don't Get Me Started"
Rhett Akins' first Grand Ole Opry performance, December 13th
Helen Darling is selected by *Country America* as Top 10 Best New Artist For 1996
Decca Label ranked # 13 in *Billboard's* "Country Singles & Tracks Labels"
Mark Wright ranked #18 *Billboard's* "Hot Singles & Tracks Producer"
Mark Wright BMI Songwriter Award for five songs that reached over one million plays
Shelia Shipley Biddy "Microsoft Chat Room" as the 3rd record industry person to ever host a national chat (Owen Bradley and Harold Bradley were the other two)

1997

Mark Chesnutt #1 in *Billboard* (two weeks), *R&R*, and *Gavin* with "It's a Little Too Late"
Mark Chesnutt #1 video with "It's a Little Too Late"
Mark Chesnutt CMT Video Artist of the Month - January
Mark Chesnutt's "Greatest Hits" is certified Gold
Mark Chesnutt's #1 Video with "Let It Rain"
Mark Chesnutt and Gary Allan selected to perform on "Crown Royal Country Music Tour"
Gary Allan #1 Video at CMT Latin America with "Forever and a Day"
"Forever and a Day" video selected as Best Country Video by the National Association of Video Producers
Gary Allan is selected by *Country America* as Top 10 Best New Artist For 1997
Gary Allan and Lee Ann Womack selected by *Country America* as only new artists featured in October issue sponsored by Chevrolet
Lee Ann Womack #1 *Billboard* Heat Seekers Chart with debut album
Lee Ann Womack Top 10 *Billboard* country album
Lee Ann Womack # 1Video on TNN with "Never Again, Again"
Lee Ann Womack first Grand Ole Opry Performance - May 31
Lee Ann Womack nominated for CMA Horizon Award - August 5
Lee Ann Womack is the first *new* artist to break Top 15 in 1997 for the first time
Lee Ann Womack is the first *new* female artists to hit #1 in 1997 for the first time
Lee Ann Womack has a Top 5 Album in Great Britain
Lee Ann Womack "The Fool" wins SESAC "1997 Song of the Year" for and estimated 500,000 plays
Lee Ann Womack "The Fool" hits #1 in *R&R*, *Gavin*, and *Gavin Only*
Lee Ann Womack "The Fool" # 1 video on TNN
Lee Ann Womack wins British CMA Award for Best International Album
Lee Ann Womack album certified Gold
Lee Ann Womack named #1 New Artist for *Billboard*
Lee Ann Womack named #1 New Female Artist for Billboard
Lee Ann Womack named #2 New Artist For *R&R* (no sales used)
Lee Ann Womack #8 (Top 10) Female Artist for *R&R* (all females)
Lee Ann Womack #10 (Top 10) Female Artist for *Billboard* (all females)
Lee Ann Womack is the *only* new artist to have a song research in Rusty Walker's Top 25 Songs For 1997 with "The Fool"
Mark Chesnutt named Top 10 (#9) Male Artist for *R&R*
Decca Records ranked 11th as label (up from 13)
Mark Chesnutt is Rusty Walker's #9 Best Testing Artist for 1997
Mark Chesnutt is the *Billboard's* 10th Most Played Video Artist for 1997
Mark Chesnutt is *R&R's* #10 Male MVP

<u>1998</u>

Lee Ann Womack American Music Award winner for Best New Country Artist
Lee Ann Womack album nominated for a Nashville Music Award for Best Country Album
Lee Ann Womack wins *Performance Magazine's* Top New Touring Artist for 1997
Mark Chesnutt appears on *David Letterman* on January 27
Lee Ann Womack opens on the George Strait 1998 Tour March 19
Shelia Shipley Biddy given Music Women's International's President's Award
Lee Ann Womack wins *Country Weekly* Best Female Newcomer
Lee Ann Womack ACM wins Best New Female Vocalist
Lee Ann Womack ACM finalist for Song of the Year, "The Fool"
Rhett Akins ACM finalist for Best New Make Artist
Chris Knight album is #1 on American Chart - March 20, 1998
Chris Knight album is #1 on American Chart for six consecutive weeks, setting a record for most weeks at #1 by a debut artist
Lee Ann Womack wins for MCN/TNN Best New Female
Shane Stockton first Grand Ole Opry performance on June 13
Lee Ann Womack finalist for Country Music Association Female Vocalist of the Year and Horizon Award (First time in ten years an act has been nominated in both categories in one year's time)
Dolly Parton is High Debut at #32 on Gavin Americana Chart, and is #1 most added with 34 first week adds for 39% of the chart the first week! August 7, 1998 issue
Mark Wright inducted into the Arkansas Entertainment Hall of Fame - October 2, 1998
Gary Allan selected by *People Magazine* as the "Sexiest Man In Country Music" - October 1998 (the previous year it was George Strait)
Gary Allan selected by *Seventeen Magazine* as the "Coolest Man in Country Music" - October 1998
Mark Chesnutt "I Don't Want to Miss a Thing" sets record for highest career debut on *R&R* at #36
Danni Leigh "If the Jukebox Took Teardrops" #1 CMT Latin America video
Lee Ann Womack wins *ABC Radio Real Country Network* "Rising Star" Award (listener voted)
Lee Ann Womack "A Little Past Little Rock" #1 single in *R&R*, *Gavin* (2 weeks), *Gavin Only*
Lee Ann Womack "A Little Past Little Rock" #1 Video on CMT
Lee Ann Womack selected as *Gavin* "Artist to Break in 1999"
Decca Records ranked #10 by *Radio & Records* for 1998's Country Label of the Year
Decca Records ranked #24 (out of 25) by *Radio & Records* for 1998's Label of the Year - All Genres Of Music

Decca Records ranked #10 by *Billboard* for 1998's Hot Country Single & Tracks Label
Decca Records nominated by *Gavin* as Country Label of the Year (only five nominations out of 27 labels)
Trudie Richardson & Enzo DeVincenzo nominated by *Gavin* as Label Reps of the Year
Lee Ann Womack is voted *Radio & Records* Female MVP for the Year (Ranked #7)
Lee Ann Womack *Billboard's* Top Country Female Artist (Ranked #8)
Mark Wright cracks *Billboard's* Top 10 Producers for the year (ranked #8) with fourteen charted singles and albums
Lee Ann Womack *Some Things I Know* album selected by *USA Today* as one of their Top 10 Country Album Picks for 1998! (Ranked #2)
Dolly Parton *Hungry Again* album selected by *USA Today* as one of their Top 10 Country Album Picks for 1998! (Ranked #6)

<u>1999</u> *(Decca closed January 21, 1999)*

Lee Ann Womack - Grammy Finalist for "Best Female Country Performance" - "A Little Past Little Rock" (a first for Decca Records and a first for Lee Ann Womack)
Mark Chesnutt celebrates his first #1 Country *Sales* Single with "I Don't Want to Miss a Thing"
Chris Knight #4 *Gavin* Americana 1998 Album of the Year
Mark Chesnutt "I Don't Want to Miss Thing" #1 in *Gavin Only* – January 22, 1999 – Spent 4 weeks at #1 in *Billboard* and *R&R*
Lee Ann Womack *Some Things I Know* and *Lee Ann Womack* certified platinum

Made in the USA
Columbia, SC
13 November 2020